Worth 6 Digits and More ™

THE CHANGE BEFORE THE DOLLARS

Nasha Barnes

Worth 6 Digits and More™
The Change Before the Dollars

ISBN: 978-09852505-0-8

Aim Higher Enterprises
P.O. Box 422
Syracuse, New York 13205

Cover Design: IAM Global Media Inc. (www.iamgminc.com)
Book Design: Lyndy McLaughlin
Author Photograph: LaVergne Harden Photography
Editor: Sondra Denise Roberts, Angela's Daughter Publishing

To India,
You are the joy of my life.

CONTENTS

Women Worth 6 Digits and More

A Worthy Journey
NASHA BARNES

In dealing with what was a life-changing circumstance, the author tells a story of how being unemployed opened doors to discover her true passion allowing her to pursue a dream. As she fights through her call to ministry, she discovers she is blessed when she becomes more obedient. Out of her lesson, she is given a gift.

This woman is fueled by the naysayers of the world and driven to help others quiet down words that can damage. Her favorite question: *Who can't?*

It was the furthest thing from her mind, but after she thought it over, she knew she made the right decision. Basketball Coach Bills says her life hasn't been the same ever since.

If you want to know the true meaning of my sister's keeper just ask this trailblazer who grew up in a time when there were no excuses.

She was raised to expect the best, so if you doubt her abilities, she will prove you wrong. The strength of this woman gets taken to another level when her son was born. See why she remains focused on keeping a positive outlook to things that wouldn't otherwise be considered good news.

Just when you think she would have had enough, her belief in God sees her through. See how she underwent what many would not be able to handle in a lifetime.

This 85 year-old wise woman gives a bit of wisdom on keeping the faith, believing, and serving as you age.

 Relinquish Your Desires
MONICA HUGHLEY

At first she thought he was not her type then she learned that she had to try something different to meet the man of her dreams.

 She Had the Vision to Do It
TAMEIKA BURRELL

She cringed at the thought of having to change her life, but she was sent a vision beyond belief that landed her in front of 10,000 people.

 She Was Finally Heard
LISA C. R.

No one ever believed that talking it out could become so freeing. This mother of two tells how she saved her family with a little couch time.

23   Be Good to Yourself
KAREN MOHAMMED

She may be a *diamond in the ruff* but this woman of God says don't it get twisted because she's been there done that. Think again!

24   She Refused to Lay Down
LORRAINE LYNCH (LADY LOE)

She was living on the dark side before an incident changed her life. What seemed like a dead end turned into never-ending light.

25   Blessed That They Call On Her
VERETTA DUDLEY

She never held her tongue before so don't think that she will now. She has regained her sensibility and will gladly tell you about it.

29   A Spiritual Awakening
VICKIE WILLIAMS

Addressing herself was the hardest thing she has had to do thus far. Her enlightenment came when she realized she was attracting the wrong people to her inner circle.

30   The Gift of Appreciation
JULIE FLANDERS

She never saw it coming but God blessed her with unexpected gifts from unexpected people to help her value herself enough to feel worthy.

31   She's Telling It
BEV JOHNSON

God was trying to tell her something but she fought it long and hard. Now this gospel recording artist/songwriter gives God all the glory for her voice of soul.

Dear Sister,

Look at what you've taught me!
To look inside myself and find the gifts God's brought me.
To keep marching on, to take the first seat on the bus,
To carve my name in diamond so that it will never rust;
And never be broken

Adversity is the token that makes me put my whole soul in...
Into jumping the barrier and reaching the top.
The world told me I couldn't so now, I'll never stop!
Never stop believing 'til my triumph reigns free!
As God as my witness they will never break me!

By: India B'nai Dancil

1 A Worthy Journey
NASHA BARNES

"What began as a circumstance,
turned into an experience, out of it came a lesson,
and now it's a gift to you from me and 30 wise women of color."

I believe that life has a way of constantly evolving us and shaping us into our predetermined destiny. I know that had I not evolved into who I am today, I don't know what my outlook may have looked like.

For certain, there were several journeys along the way. They are now a part of my history. I wish I could tell you that I was all done growing, but I'm not. I'm still evolving, still trying to figure it out, and enjoying the ride. This particular journey is nothing more than a snippet of a moment in time when I confirmed that I truly was *Worth 6 Digits and More.*

THE CIRCUMSTANCE

It started early in 2009. I was let go from a position within a company awarded as a wonderful place to work. There were a lot of miracles that happened to get me there in the first place. I had transitioned through the company in a few different positions and I really felt as though God had answered my prayers – I was given a dream opportunity.

Several years ago when I was completing my undergraduate degree as a non-traditional student, I had an assignment to write down what my ideal opportunity would look like. It had no title, but it had specific requirements. Years later, I happened to find the job description while cleaning my home. That's when I realized; my dream list still remains the same to date. This is what I would love to do.

It was called a Tradeshow, Event and Meeting Specialist. But it was more than that. I was the person who checked the branding out in the field, who represented the company, and who interacted with the customers. I spoke to people to gain an understanding of what they needed, what they wanted, and how they felt about the product and service. It was my job to learn about how people viewed the company and to assist them with making the best choices – that's what I did.

I like to be up close and personal with people, I like stories. I especially love to hear stories of where we come from and the history of how things came about. I have my saying, "Once you determine a person's baggage (history), then it all makes sense from there." It really does. We are all a collection of our encounters in life and it makes us who we are. That's what makes us unique and of different mindsets as a whole.

In that company, I was a person who could build relationships internally and externally; a person who could cross many lines if you will. I was there for four years. It was an international company that allowed me to meet many people and build several friendships. I was flexible and had an eagerness to grow. I will admit that I am a go-getter, a person who believes in action. Like many, I am truly afraid of failure, but I also believe that if you do what you always did, you'll get what you always got and you'll be who you always were. – and if you don't try, you've already failed, so I don't believe in giving in and giving up on myself before I have even tried. I believe that when we try, if that thing doesn't work, it may lead us to the next thing that may be even bigger and better for us. As this was such the case with me. I was let go asking, "God, really? I thought this was my dream opportunity and you gave it to me and so what else do I do after this?"

Truly, the company offered me the ability to travel around the world, to connect with many, to learn a lot, to provide for my family, it was going to allow me to have a great future. The only logical thing it meant to me was there was something more that I had to do. It was being an entrepreneur. This was something that I wanted to be as early as the age of 18. I've always had big visions, and big dreams of owning my own company. I would be that speaker, that mentor, that person helping people find their way by offering them leadership in their lives. So, there I was faced with unemployment and I had the opportunity to figure out what I wanted to do. Whether that meant find another position, or reinvent myself, I honestly had no fear or worries. It was probably the most peaceful time in my life to know that God had released me. There was something much greater out there for me.

A Worthy Journey

The time had come to figure out what that something was. I really wasn't worried about money. I wasn't concerned with home, food, or how I would live; I had family that was there to help me. I'm thankful for my family, especially my grandmother. So those were not pressing issues of mine. My daughter was taken care of. She was still overseas in Switzerland at the time and I was going to make sure that she was okay as she fulfilled her assignment as an international exchange student ambassador for our country.

So, I placed it out there, because I believe when you speak aloud that's the only way to truly be heard bringing life to your thoughts. I was now in my last semester of graduate school, graduating with my MBA and I came to realize later on that the company was not supposed to be my final destination. Rather, it was the stepping stone that I needed to help me receive the true blessing. If you think you've got it all figured out and can see the vision to the end then you really truly need to re-examine your faith, because God will show you that He will deliver more to you than you can even imagine. So believe He will.

I was in class and telling a friend what happened. She asked me what I wanted to do and I told her that I just wanted to volunteer my time -- go back to the community that I was raised in and give back expertise to those who could use it. I had been living in the suburbs, and traveling about the country for about four years so it was time and I always wanted to be a teacher. So she said, "Okay let me see what I can do for you." Before I knew it she gave me the name of a woman named Monica and sent me to a business center in the City of Syracuse. I went there and met the woman and was very happy, because my friend who sent me there looked like me and so did she—a woman of color. In my small city there aren't large pools of visible professional black women. I knew immediately we would connect just because I believed.

There I was with an open mind, trying to see what this center was all about. I hadn't heard about it nor seen the building before. Monica gave me the tour, yet I still didn't feel a connection. I had the utmost respect for her, her director position, and all that she had shared about the center, but I couldn't see myself fitting in. I couldn't see beyond the walls what I could contribute as a service to the incubator full of entrepreneurs. But as my meeting was ending, her phone rang and it was her daughter. I tried not to listen to the conversation although I learned that her daughter was preparing for college the next year. Soon thereafter she got off the call and I asked her about her daughter. I ended up sharing with her that I had a daughter in college and that she was actually oversees and just about to return to start college in New York City. Immediately, we clicked and we bonded on that topic among others. We had several stories to share about being mothers, uplifting our children, being that leader in each of their lives, the community, the needs of our people, and eventually how the center could use my help.

The connection was made and before I knew it she asked me to come back the following week for a meeting with other staff members and to learn a little bit more. After I left, I prepared myself for a possible volunteer's role and to my surprise; I came in to meet a table full of women. I quickly found out that they were counselors at the center and before I knew it we were scheduling our work assignments. Monica then said to me, "You need to go up to human resources and fill out your paperwork. You do get paid for this you know." Now I was thinking, wait a minute, I have a job? I was oblivious and God has presented to me bigger than I expected -- I had been hired as a part-time business counselor. I had a job. It was flexible and automatically I felt like a contractor. I felt like it was setting me up as an entrepreneur doing freelance work. It was an awesome opportunity.

A number of months later, Monica left the company and I continued on working in the women's division of the business center. The position grew as more grants came through and I was eventually offered more hours, which then placed me over the allotment for unemployment. With the new grant I assumed the role as the center navigator, as well as a business counselor.

In May 2010, after being at the center for about a year and a half, I was asked to assist a local woman pastor who had shown interest in working with the center. The center's outreach director at the time had developed a relationship with community organizations and local churches. The pastor decided to pursue the opportunity; she was in search of a way to help women members of her congregation and other women leaders in her program with starting a business. I was asked to design a program to help them learn how to take their God given talents to the next level. I designed a four-week program in a matter of an hour. I was able to see the vision pretty quickly as to how this could work and how we could make it interactive. I wrote this for this pastor as well as for the director of the woman's business center and remember saying, "Here you go."

Well, it turned out that they had no intentions of teaching the course; it was for me to teach. I guess I was quite stunned, because I had not realized that I had designed the program for me, but thought I was handing it over per their request. I can say that it caused a lot of turmoil for me internally. In particular, because it was teaching women who in my mind would be strongly-judging women of faith. This was after all designed to be a business course for faith-based women.

I didn't feel qualified to teach the women. Why? Because I shifted through different religions and beliefs. I had always kept my faith strong as I came from a very strong faith-based family.

I honestly felt like there were certain qualifiers to teach faith-based people – this was my perception. I thought I needed to know scripture, be versed and know the lingo, dress a certain way, and be active in a church. I thought I would be viewed a certain way. These are things that were in my mind. They were my perceptions. I didn't know. This was the misconception that I had about faith-based people. At the time, I actually believed that they would be almost perfect. That meant they would crucify me - I just didn't know.

I had recently started my faith walk seriously and had joined a church about a year prior to that. I had been baptized for years, but not attending service or committing to my walk with Christ. To me, I was learning, I was loving, I was grasping, I was acknowledging God's glory, I was getting the ah-ha moment of the truth behind the place of worship and God's children. I was getting to a place of understanding that we're not a perfect people; that we have the ability to mask because we look so well, dress so well, speak so well.

And so I thought, wait a minute, these are the people that are coming to my class. These are the people that I'm supposed to stand in front of? How will they view me? How will I be judged and what will it be based on? It took me a moment to remember that I was teaching a business course and they were just another audience of people. It was not a religious course; they were women, everyday women, who were joined together by faith and spirituality. They were no different than anyone else in most respects, except they believed in a higher power. They had an extra support system that couldn't be seen but could be witnessed. They walked the line a little straighter.

What was I afraid of? I wasn't sure, but it mattered. So I had to meditate and pray on that but it still caused me tremendous anxiety before the class started. I had not slept for four days prior to teaching the class, I was nervous. I had so many thoughts going through my head: How would they learn to trust me? Why do I feel like this is so different than anything else I've done? I have taught classes around the country, why in the world am I tripping? I have taught CEOs, the best of the best, government officials, you name it and now I want to be timid?

THE LESSON

I was about to teach women that I believed to be holy. Considering them to be holier than thou -- and that was my mistake. The pastor came in a little early before the class and she knew me, so she asked me, "What's wrong with you?" and I looked at her and said, "Nothing." She asked me again, "What's wrong with you?" and I said that I hadn't slept in days. When she asked me why not, I recall saying that I didn't want to do it, I didn't think I was supposed to be the one to teach the class. That was something that I would never have chosen and I felt a certain kind of way.

She said, "Okay, okay. Can we go in a room and talk privately?" So we went in a conference room and I began to tell her what my fear was. I told her I wanted to be able to do my job, I just wanted to be able to connect with them and I wanted the prejudgments to be gone. That is why I hadn't volunteered in a church, because I didn't want to get caught up, I simply wanted to do what I do and know what God sent me to do, and I was going on and on and on. And she laughed at me. Then she grabbed my hands and said, "Let us pray." I laughed out loud, tickled in an outburst by her attempt to save me. I was thinking what was she going to say? But, her words – I listened, and I listened very intensely to the words of prayer. She prayed for me and I heard her say words that I had heard before out of other pastor's mouths. Until then, I never really paid attention to the prayers' actual meaning.

The first thing I heard her say was:
"Lord, let your voice be heard. Let Nasha decrease and You increase.

A Worthy Journey

Deliver the words to her so that they may be heard; deliver the words to her as you would have them. Bring her comfort, bring her peace..."

Then, there was an overwhelming feeling that's hard to explain. But I will say the Lord took over and I was elated. I had been replaced and was no longer standing there by myself. I was standing there with Him. Before me was a group of spiritual women, they all had ministries embedded in them, and they came to learn about business and I was ready to speak to them.

I came out and greeted them, and everyone was grabbing a bite to eat before we began. I realized at that time that it was a diverse room and not quite what I had imagined. Some had blue eyes, blonde hair, some were dressed, some were queens and first ladies and the list goes on. I knew that my perception was blown again. I had made a determination about what a spiritual woman of faith looked like and knew that I was learning while I stood there.

In front of the room, I grabbed the attention of the class that consisted of approximately 33 people. I started to instruct as I always did when teaching any class, but I realized the minute I opened my mouth the words that came out were not my own. I could hear me and control what I was saying to a certain extent, but that voice was not my own, that diction was not my own, thoughts came to me that were not my own, that rhythm was not my own. There was a calmness about me that made me feel like I was literally ministering to these women, reaching and connecting to them and I remember looking out and seeing their eyes, and faces asphyxiated on my every word.

They had these stares and I had never taught a class that had a gaze so penetrating. I then relaxed in it. I knew that God had me and this was His time. Whatever I was meant to teach was going to come through. I no longer needed to worry about saying the right thing and the rest followed. It was done.

The class went on, and another class continued. A year later, I was still the teacher and the business counselor to the women of faith. I held one-on-one private sessions with them for about an hour per week helping each one individually strategize their business goals. The 30+ group of women grew to 70. They began to trust me, telling me their biggest fears, largest obstacles, faith positions, family situations, and career situations. I ended up becoming their business counselor, career coach, confidant, mentor and nurturer – all in one. I had become proficient in my skill and I'll be honest in saying there were a few scary moments for me. I started to get good if you know what mean. I started to live in the moment, and could feel and almost predict what the outcome would be. I could get right to the root cause more quickly and I loved doing what I did.

As a counselor, I started realizing my women needed couch time, which makes me laugh just typing this. But don't we all from time to time. They knew to come to me and they knew I would listen. In couch time they would have outburst, crying outbursts to be exact. This is the first time I'm actually revealing this, but it is what it is. It was okay, but the first time it really took me by surprise. I wasn't really sure what to do with a woman whose soul was coming out as she explained to me how she hadn't been able to release that part of herself to anyone because of how they may view her. There was a part of history that had blocked her from moving forward and that was too scary to reveal to people for sake that they may interpret it as a weakness. It would make her look like a woman that was less than what she was.

She had masked and put out an image of a strong, unbreakable, courageous presence out here, and underneath it all she was still human. She still had a need, and in some areas she was powerless, her belief was not strong enough, her faith was not strong enough. That was something that she needed to fight for. That was something that she couldn't get through alone because she couldn't admit it to anyone. So how did she get passed this? Yes, she called on God, but at that point she needed to talk. She needed face-to-face time with another woman who could literally help her with steps to get through. She had God on her side, but needed a woman of faith to help her face her reality.

That's when the counseling took a turn. I realized, that was some type of ministry. I was sitting there and the women began to call me a minister and they began to say that was my ministry. They said that is what I was called to do. To me it felt like here I go again in another spin of evolution -- I never considered myself ministering to anyone nor being called a minister. But I knew subconsciously that I was at that point. I was a non-traditional minister.

I never thought about having a ministry. I've always called it just helping people. People have been coming to me practically my entire life, ever since I was a young girl. People have come to me for counseling, wanting for me to move them through hindrances in their lives. It has always been one-on-one, so there was a time when I just thought they were friends. That's what I called them anyway. They got what they got and went on. That was a painful reality to me prior to discovering my line of ministry, because I could never understand why after people friended me and used my help, they would then leave. I remember feeling in life that every time I helped somebody for whatever reason, they moved or left. So, for me helping people became a painful experience.

So there I was, and the women that I counseled were calling me their business counselor and friend. They said that was my ministry and that I was ministering to them. They were actually coming to me to minister to them. I was a little stuck on the terminology I think, but at the same time I embraced it. I said, "Well God if this is what you're pushing me a little further to do then so be it. We'll do this thing."

And so I took it one day at a time, not even week by week, but day by day. I tell you each day I got dressed invigorated to go to work, I couldn't wait to meet with the women and then the women started to send me more; more of their friends and business partners from all over the place. I once had a woman who came for counseling, and someone in the office said, "I think she belongs with you." I questioned why. Due to her type of business, she wouldn't have normally been assigned to me (she had a wellness and healing business). Yet I agreed to take her in. She was a very spiritual woman and we had an immediate connection. Before I knew it God sent me anyone who needed me. I had women referring other women as far as two hours away who were willing to drive the distance just to meet with me. Yes, we got to the next level of their business and yes we had some breakthroughs in their lives. Yes, we got over some barriers and yes some humps. Yes, I helped them with their marketing and branding and yes I allowed them to be who they were—their authentic spiritual selves. I told them, "Let those who are looking for your product or service find you and stand strong in the gifts and talents that God gave you. Claim it and own it." And they did. To date, there are around 300+ women that I've helped and from city to city they come.

It wasn't long before the ministry and business counseling took another turn and began to extend outside of the center. I was welcomed into people's homes to meet with them and held meetings at coffee shops. Some women didn't want to be on record anymore at the center and wanted our sessions to be more confidential. From there it continued. I realized that every conversation I had with women became about their authentic selves, their hindrances of their lives, and surpassing their own expectations. The focus became about taking their dreams to the next level.

Not long afterwards I sat down with the pastor and we had a recap. Somehow we fast forward to her asking me, 'So when are you starting your company?' I laughed at her and said, "Yeah that's always been in the back of my head." But I knew I could no longer stand before the class and push them to do the difficult if I hadn't done it myself. I truly believed in myself, but just didn't feel I was ready. But we made a pact and I said, "Okay it is done – by end of year." She replied, "No, next week." She actually gave me a date and I remember feeling that it was too soon, too fast, she had just raised the bar on me – I guess like I did to the women. But I needed that. She told me what I was going to do: to send my company name to her and have it registered the following week. I thought umph okay. So I left her and I was in a fog, a daze, some other cloud.

I drove home, but couldn't remember how I got there. My mind was gone and I was asking myself is this the time? I couldn't believe it was about to happen. It was a little too spontaneous for me. What I really needed to ask myself was what I am I afraid of?

I knew that it wasn't about validation, or was it? I had lived my whole life fearing that I wasn't good enough, always trying to get every single goal accomplished and checking off every box for completeness.

I believed if you allowed people to place you in a compartment (a box) you'll always have to validate your skill set, your talent, your gift, your being, you will never attain anything because there's always another measure coming out; another check box to be filled. The minute that you complete that one, there's another one. You go for the two-year degree and then there's someone telling you that you need a four-year or a graduate degree, or before you know it now you need 10 years of experience, or cross-training in three different areas along with that. Then you need to be referred by someone they know, it's a never ending list. At some point you need to ask who is out here developing this checklist of requirements for success when truly you know you can learn to do the job from the next person or just be born to do it, because of innate ability that God has given you. I cast down being validated based on a checklist of requirements – I am done – I knew I was worthy.

Within a few days, I registered my business Aim Higher Enterprises. I had taken all that I had experienced in life to formulate the company name. It said it all.

I learned a lot about myself from this incident and I tell others all the time to *perfect your craft, stay studied up, be versed in others opinions so that you have one, and stand your ground. Know what you can know to avoid as many pitfalls as you can that can become hindrances.*

Most of all do not allow these check boxes to constantly keep you down from building on your dreams and obtaining what it is you think God has for you. Follow your gut, instinct, your sixth sense, your spirit of where He sent you. Follow the gifts and talents that He's applied in you. Follow them. What are you afraid of?

THE EXPERIENCE

And so out of all of that came this book. I woke up one morning with a thought and a dream. I had a dream that I was being sent to Atlanta and I was uncertain why. This came after I was told that my part-time counseling position may end at the end of July. I was told that I may not have a job and that I could expect my last day to be July 31, 2011. I don't know what that did to my mindset, but it immediately put me in a position of thinking okay I have started this business but I haven't really taken it to the level that I could. I have allowed myself to be here teaching, and still a little complacent in some other areas. So again I needed to focus a little more on myself, instead of focusing on other things. Yet in all I knew it was a life lesson and that I was where I was supposed to be.

One morning at the end of August 2011, I clearly remember waking up saying, "Wow here I go, I've had a month of not working and a month of being on unemployment again." And yes, I was still out doing things in the community and being actively involved even at the center under small contracts, but I couldn't forget the dream that I had. The message in the dream was that I was going to Atlanta, I had no clue why. I couldn't figure out heads or tails. I argued with myself out loud and I argued with God. The thought didn't make any sense nor would it make sense to anyone else if I had to explain it. But I needed to go. My unemployment check had come; I looked online to see that low and behold there was a discounted ticket for $188.00 directly from Syracuse to Atlanta; and I knew right then that was my blessing.

A Worthy Journey

I had asked people for support and they were more than willing to help me
do what I needed without question. But I knew I needed to move quickly,
so I decided to do things myself and bypass the help. I have this spirit of
action; I had no time to waste and I needed to make sure that it happened.
That was my feeling – I was getting it done.

So I went to Atlanta and I brought a huge suitcase. I remember my family
asking if I was staying for good? I had business suits in there, leisure
clothes, and it was going to be 80 degrees outside. I really had no clue if
I was doing business there, meeting with organizations and networking,
teaching or what. I just kept asking God, "What am I doing here?" Soon as
I landed, I took a picture where I look like I was about 12 years old, really
scared with a lost face. I tried to smile right through it but underneath
there was so much uncertainty. But as I left the large airport and stepped
outside to wait for my family, as soon as I saw the sunshine I had an
overwhelming feeling that let me know I was where I needed to be. It felt
like home.

I know that every question that I asked God about the journey was
answered, except for why I was there. There was even a point where I
believed I heard him say I was moving there; relocating. So, I don't know,
maybe I took the word move out of context, and maybe it meant you are
on the move. Moving, on the move, it's time for you to move – it has yet
to be determined. Who knows if I placed move in the right context of my
hearing and understanding. I do know that I moved my behind and I got
there.

The night of arrival my cousin told me that we were going to a house party of some friends in another area. He said he just told them all that he was bringing his cousin from New York with no other info. So I got ready for a party/cook out and I was dressed casual. I was ready to relax, but I had my business cards in my purse just in case.

Once we got there the women were preparing the dishes in the house and the men were in the back on the grill. Trying to mingle but not really saying too much of anything, I sat observing and sipping on a drink that they had given me. I ended up sitting at the table with the hostess' sister. She looked at me and asked what I thought about ATL? And I said, "Well, I haven't seen it yet, I just got here today, but so far so good. So she replied, "What are doing here?" All I could do was just look at her. She said, "I know you're going to think I'm crazy but I have to tell you something and please don't look at me like I'm nuts." And I agreed that I wouldn't. She proceeds to tell me that God gave her a word to give me and that word was that I was needed there. And that I was in the right place and that God said to her the women there needed me and what I do. I took a deep breath and then she asked, "What do you do?"

I was speechless trying to figure out how do I answer that question right now. I still was not totally comfortable saying what I do, to people who didn't know me. So I didn't say much of anything. By that point she had asked me if I was a minister? I was really confused wondering where she was getting her questions from? I was sitting there with shorts and a t-shirt on, so how did she see that I might be some kind of minister, with a drink in my hand no less. She said, "You are aren't you?" I just said, "I guess you can say something like that. Some say I have a ministry." I still hadn't fully claimed it outwardly yet, but I told her what I do.

A Worthy Journey

She got extremely excited and before I knew it she was telling every woman in the room. Then they all began to huddle around me and now we were talking business and we're talking about dreams and visions, and how I can help them. We were speaking about faith and they wanted me to come to their churches and meet with their pastors and women's ministries while I was there – to start my program in their communities. It was a night full of helping all the women, some with business counseling and helping them get them off the ground, or advice on taking them to the next level. Another, I was her coach in helping her to pass her board exam and finding creative ways for her to overcome the test and I was in awe with what God was showing me. I began to believe that was one of the reasons why I was there.

The story continues with many other women that were placed in my path for me to connect with. In fact, the very next morning the phone rang at 8 o'clock with an unknown woman's voice on the other line letting me know that I didn't know her, but that she got my contact info from someone else that I helped. She let me know that my number had gone viral and was out there and several women would be calling to meet with me while I was in town. She also let me know that she was going to act as my organizer and put together group calls and meetings to make it easier on me because the need was so great. I was beside myself. That week I had over 70 women that I encountered and offered assistance to. I began to understand my reasons for being there, learning the profile of Atlanta and the needs of the women I spoke with.

Out of that experience the vision got greater and I knew I needed to do more. I started speaking to the women about ideas and the excitement spread. I soon left Atlanta and journeyed a few weeks later to the Congressional Black Caucus in Washington, D.C. and then to the Woman Thou Art Loosed Conference in Texas. It was the grace of God that I was able to attend these events as angels surrounded my every path making a way for me to attend and placing people in my life that I would re-connect with at a later date. At each event, I spoke life into my vision that God placed on my heart, doors opened, and I was heard. I was more motivated than ever before to see my projects through.

I came home and began to plan. It was in the planning stages sometime in October 2011 when I began to see a little clearer. There was a lot of work to be done to complete my projects, but I felt God was refining what I was doing. It was Him saying to me, I do want you to speak to women on a platform, I do want you to continue to connect women with expert resources from all over, but more importantly, you need to tell your story about this journey. And you need to connect with women on a larger scale rather than just Atlanta.

I thought, Lord how will I do that, what am I supposed to do to make this happen? I thought about it and started strategically planning allowing the vision to just grow. It's humorous now, but that's not exactly what He had in store. I could tell when I got stuck that nope, I didn't get it, and I wasn't listening. So I listened a little bit more and I was lost. I put everything down for about a week and I started studying a little bit more going back to what I knew. I didn't know anything else except to go back and study the word.

I picked up my Bible that I hadn't seen in a minute, except you know when I was in church on Sundays. So I started reading again and I ended up in Proverbs, which I had been in before. But this time I started at the beginning of the chapter, reading over the intro and it was like the words were a magnet to my eyes. The words that I read aloud were a melody to my ears. The reading was a rhythm to my soul. They jumped off the page in 3D and I immediately knew that I was out here reaching what we call the ideal woman.

It came to me that I needed to write and tell their stories and help people get through their hindrances and connect women across the world before I started on my next projects. I asked God to show me the vision a little more clearly, because I wasn't trying to write a thing at the moment. I hadn't written in book format since I was about 18, back in 1988 when I was in my freshman year of college for Journalism. I couldn't believe that's what I was doing. But you know what, every day it became so vivid and so concise and as I continued reading I stumbled over the words – worthiness.

It narrowed down to everything I had worried about and everything I do. I'm helping people understand their self-worth and that's what I've been doing all my life – confirming. I knew that was it. I had a special gift to help more women than men because that's who I place myself around and that's who He has sent to me.

I went into high-gear studying and praying and looking for the ability to discern what He was truly trying to say to me. I was asking him again, how would I do this? What am I doing? Why am I doing this now? Asking if that's what this whole lesson has been about; to heal and transition women. But now I understand that I must go worldly, must go big. I laughed and I said, "God you never have me do anything small. But okay if you believe in me, than it shall be done."

I prayed on it because I had concentrated on all of Proverbs, which has 31 chapters, and I was led to the ideal woman in Proverbs 31. I knew it was meant for me to tell the stories of 31 women. But I didn't know 31 women who would fit the profile. I went to a revival and received a word and the Reverend prayed that all blessings would be given in the next two days. Within two days God sent me a friend that I hadn't connected with in a long while. This man unconditionally gave me a list of women that he knew personally. I was well on my way. Out of the 31 women, he sent me 15. I knew 9 that I had met along the way, and the rest came through the other women. God showed up on time.

Then the title came to me as, "Worth 6 Digits and More," because we are constantly hearing about ourselves in terms of monetary worth and how much money we make, types of positions we have, and titles and statuses that we carry. I knew that even if I wanted to attain that six-digit, six-figure salary, there's something so much more significant about placing value on yourself. Where you find yourself within those words represents the actual change that you've encountered before any dollar can be placed in your hand. I finally got it.

It's not about how much you make or what you do; that does not equate to what you're worth. The two are distinctly different and we need to begin to understand that our worth is so much more complex than that. Our most common mistake is that we place value on ourselves in the eyes of others, instead of in the eyes of God. Maybe we don't realize that we were already born worthy. We've been given everything we needed from day one –we are complete. Worth is nothing anyone can take from you. Your value that's within you is yours. Why do we continually give it away allowing someone to strip us of it? The harsh reality is that I am referring to everyone from our mate, to any person we have a relationship with, and that includes your parents, it can include those that are taking care of you, or a relative. It can be an educator, teacher, professor, a boss, a coworker, or a friend – anyone human. So, if people in your lives or who come across your lives aren't sharing positive encouragement and building your esteem up, then stop allowing that other human being to dictate to you, your level of worth.

THE GIFT

If you take something from this book let it be this – here are 31 women, each who are as you are, already the ideal woman just because. I have told you, it doesn't matter about the setbacks and hindrances you've had. We all have them, many of them. When I asked the women to tell me a story about worthiness and how it played a role in their lives, they could tell me 5, 10, and 15 stories, but I had to choose one. I wanted to show you that things do happen to us all and you'll be able to connect to some of the situations in some way, shape or form. And although these women work hard for money and fame, they are successful *merely* because they have a good reputation, moral character and the spiritual devotion to obey Him.

You will see through them that if not for any other reason; if you can relate to a similar situation or you're at a crossroads, hopefully this may encourage – you too, to act on them!

Remember once again that you are not isolated in your circumstances; however you are still responsible for your character. So if you keep your reputation good, keep it in the forefront and know where you came from, you'll be able to overcome these momentary trials and tribulations in your life.

Eventually, you'll grow from the lesson and you'll be able to pass it on. The lessons here are put here to show you nothing more than someone who is making it, has made it and who is still striving to make it someplace else.

A Worthy Journey

Those things have helped them change and become who they are today. Through that change they were able to obtain knowledge and go after the next thing building wisdom. So we have to continually step over these things that happen to us and remember that they're all a part of the journey and that's it. When you have a journey, you tell it. Keeping your journey locked up keeps you from growing. The women here are not perfect because there's no such thing as a perfect being. They're what you call ideal. Ideal is what we aspire to be like. We aspire to learn through our journeys no matter the magnitude. We aspire to learn about ourselves, continuing to grow so that we can nurture and help the next.

I chose to dedicate this book specifically to women of color because our history has been one where we share and learn through storytelling. It is a part of our culture to exchange lessons learned through years of stories passed down from our ancestors. It's about not being afraid to lay it on the table and say yes, you know what I've been here, and many have been here before me.

So I share among you the lesson that I've learned; the story of my past incidents. From this I have gained wisdom that allows me to pass it on to you so that you may become wiser in your decisions, more wise in your knowing, awareness, ability, faith, and more.

All the women in this book gave a part of their life memories to help you. Yes, this book relates to everyone, but it's a collective memoir of wise women of color, our stories, our triumphs, and our lessons. It's our gift to you in the form of stories.

I hope that you enjoy it.
Blessings and Glory

~ Nasha

2   **You Can Dream Big**
MELANIE LITTLEJOHN

By all accounts the odds were against her as a little black girl from South East Jamaica, Queens. As the pundits suggest, she wasn't supposed to make it out. It was her senior year in high school and time to make the big decision. She was excited. On that day, she walked into her guidance counselor's office to talk about her college choices and she walked out being told that she should consider beauty school instead.

She was told, "I don't necessarily know if you're cut out for college." Her only thought was, "Really?" She was 17 at the time, did an about-face and walked out of there with this "funky feeling" about what she had just heard. She wasn't sure why, but she knew something wasn't right. The notion of not attending college or more importantly, not being good enough, was contrary to the values instilled by her parents. It's a good thing that she had a loving and supportive relationship with her parents because it was strength that helped sustain her self-esteem.

Little did Melanie realize that would be one of her most pivotal life events. It would be the event that drove her to succeed. She needed to prove to the counselor as well as herself that she had what it took to reverse the odds and shake up the expectations that little black girls weren't good enough. Fueled by the words, you can't, Melanie went to Stony Brook graduating in three years instead of four. She says, "That was a huge moment where she recognized, that she could, and she did! If not for her internal moxie and supportive parents she could have chosen a different path.

That incident set the stage for her journey to come. Ignited by the attitude sought to marginalize her, she used the self-doubt of others to be the energy to help persevere. She said it became the guide for her life. "When girls dream big, it's easy for others to be naysayers – when black girls dream big, many underestimate and under value her potential…her voice often goes unnoticed."

Few things have been easy for Melanie. This go-getter has worked many years building her career. Notably, her work in the non-profit arena had the most profound impact on both her professional and personal life. During her years in human service she felt compelled to "give voice to the voiceless" and to "give encouragement and tools to those who felt disenfranchised, misunderstood and disrespected." At no other time in her career can she recall the sense of empowerment and purpose. She felt as though it was her duty to help provide the resources and most importantly, the encouragement to help others find their way. "There is great comfort in knowing that in some small way you help someone find and tap into their potential." She says that it was her hope that the environment she fostered was a breeding ground for positive energy. "When respect, trust and value exist, there's no room for the defeating attitude of I CAN'T only… I WILL!" declares Melanie.

Currently, Melanie works in Corporate America, a place that is all together different than the non-profit sector. She contends that the corporate environment is not for the faint of heart and that one can easily walk out a different person than when he or she walked in. "It can be a battle ground for the you can't mentality but is also a proving ground for the *I can and I will and I did* way of thinking. It can be a place to build your strength and gain confidence in your ability. In order to gain that stride, women need women who understand their trials and the importance of their triumphs. Your soul sisters are there to help squelch the voice of self-doubt. We all have them, need them and connect to them spiritually – they make the difference."

Throughout her career she's held the title many times as a first. However, her appointment as the first Black woman vice president in her corporation's history in 2005 was significant. Melanie said she asked herself, "What does this role mean? What do I do with my access and how can I use it to do good?" She committed to sharing her resources and information with people who might not otherwise have access. She also believes it's critical to share with young adults the benefits of her experience. "So that they will know how to battle back the you can't attitude – this becomes Mission Central."

Melanie reminds us that, "The walk is never straight. You think you're supposed to do one thing, and you end up finding out it was His plan, not my plan." She lives her life trying to be obedient, but from time to time, like anyone else she has the inclination to run… but she doesn't.

MEET THIS WISE WOMAN OF COLOR:

It may take a village to raise a child, but Melanie Littlejohn's parents raised 26 children in their modest home in Jamaica, New York "When my younger brother and I were in high school, my parents took in and raised twenty-four foster children, all of them girls," says Littlejohn, Regional Executive Director at National Grid, a global energy provider. "My parents did it for the love of children, but it also helped me grow up with a sense of community and purpose."

Littlejohn joined National Grid in 1994. Using her innate soft skills and emotional intelligence, she successfully tackled projects no one else wanted. Today, she is responsible for commercial and industrial customer account management, including customer satisfaction, and for managing external relationships with community leaders, organizations and local business associations. She is a trusted advisor for National Grid's largest customers and helps to create energy solutions to make businesses become more competitive. Because of her ability to connect with others and resolve issues, many see her as an ally and a resource. "When you can use your emotional intelligence to connect with someone on a very basic, human level, then you can get anything done," says Littlejohn, who has a B.A. in liberal arts from SUNY Stonybrook and an MBA from Syracuse University.

For several years, Littlejohn served as the facilitator for the Community Wide Dialogue to End Racism, a group of discussion circles started by the Interfaith Works of Central New York in Syracuse in 1997. She received the 2010 NAACP Freedom Award for her work with the Dialogue. She also received the dubious honor of being awarded as one of the "25 Most Influential Black Women in Business" award from the Network Journal in 2010.

Melanie shared a motto that she adopted from her college roommate and it has become her life's mantra… "Don't let people live in your head rent free."

3 The Ball's In Your Court
BILLIE HARRIS

Billie is a women's basketball coach at Coppin State University, but her journey didn't begin there. She's had an athletic background since after college, but she's always worked in sports divisions with men. She's been in a total man's environment where she coached men, and celebrated men, as far back as the military and on as she recalls.

She was used to them, having to deal with their point of view on everything and anything. She says she must admit though that it was more productive working with men, and it taught her a lot in due time.

She shifted over when one of the coaches told her about an open position in the women division. He told her that she had the history and a lot to contribute as a coach, then he asked her why she was still coaching men when they already had so much. He said, 'You should give your all to the women, you're a woman.' She had to give it some thought. She says, she knew he was right, but she also knew that dealing with women brought issues that they go through; and that was why she chose to coach men from the beginning. Billie believes that she's a very tactical coach and women put themselves through things that she just didn't want to handle. But she went home and slept on it. Ultimately, she made the decision to cross-over to women's basketball. She says, "It was an, ah-ha moment," and she draws back on that when she needs to get strength.

What Billie learned by working between the two divisions is there is a different way to motivate the players. On the psyche side, men require you to challenge their ego and masculinity. A simple, are you going to let someone punk you?... always works and you get results. With women, you have to pull out there assets and show them how they can get it done. She says their spirits are different. Women tend to tolerate with a thick skin for a while, but over time, when they're done, they're done.

She has been the only woman coach on her teams for a while, so she's often had to be the motivator, the momma, and coach. She can't place judgment on them, because after all you can never tell what background they've come from or what type of social upbringing they've had. Many times the young ladies, most of whom are 17-18 years old, just want to be nurtured.

Billie has to remember at all times, the ladies are diverse in every way. The bottom line she says is it's someone's child and she's come to her to be taken care of regardless of lifestyle, background or foundation. She says that she was tested a few years back when students were being manipulated. She had to raise above all the chaos and be there for the ladies' ears. She had to have the resilience to pull through; regardless if they tried to make her look like the crazy woman for standing up. She knew she was needed, so she stayed in the toxic environment. She also knew that her sense of character and faith are the only two things that sustained her. She made it through the male dominated department.

Bills, as her girls named her, feels blessed when the students come back to her for help moving forward in their careers. Some need references and others need a temporary place to stay while awaiting a tour overseas. She says that her reward is that they come back; they trust her. She says she always tells them for the road, "You have this in you, know what you have. Don't let toxic people get a hold of you and bring you down. Bring out your best asset and let them see you."

MEET THIS WISE WOMAN OF COLOR:

Billie Wilson begins her 14th season with the team and ninth as associate head basketball coach at Coppin State.

She's a member of the NCAA Black Coaches and Administrators (BCA) National Organization and recent selected member of the 2010 (BCA) Achieving Coaching Excellence Program (ACE).

A 1984 graduate of Frostburg State University, Wilson brings an extensive coaching background to the Eagle staff. She was head coach at Columbia Union College in 1994-95 and served as head coach of In Flight, a women's semi-professional team, for four years prior to coming to Coppin State.

As the primary recruiting coordinator for Coppin State, Wilson has helped recruit and develop two Players of the Year and a Rookie of the Year along with numerous other all-conference picks. She has been vital to the success of the Eagles program as the seniors of the 2004-05 MEAC Championship squad was her first recruiting class.

A native of Washington, D.C., Wilson has coached several Amateur Athletic Union teams and was named AAU National Coach of the Year in 1997.

Several of the athletes Wilson has mentored are current or former WNBA players, such as Jessie Hicks, Tari Phillips, Monique Ambers, Nikki Teasley, and Penny Moore.

During her playing days, Wilson was an All-Metro performer at Elizabeth Seton High School in Bladensburg, Maryland. The former Roadrunner star was a two-time first-team All-Catholic League selection as a junior and senior and also played in the McDonald's Capital Classic following her senior year.

She went on to star at Frostburg State and scored 1,096 points during her four-year career, earning Kodak Division III All-American honors as a senior.

Wilson received a B.S. in speech communication and theater from Frostburg in 1984 and is a member of Alpha Kappa Alpha Sorority, Inc. She currently serves as the on-campus graduate advisor of AKA at Coppin State.

After graduation, Wilson went on to work for the Department of Defense in Germany from 1985-90. During her time in Germany she worked as the intramurals director. She also served as the director and planner of all of the Army Conference events such as men's and women's basketball, softball, wrestling, boxing, and golf. She also played for the Army and Air Force women's basketball teams.

She continued her service in the USA while working for Walter Reed Army Medical Center. At WRAMC she planned a tackle football program and adult NSA athletic leagues as the assistant athletic director in charge of intramurals.

Wilson and her husband, Rowlen, have two daughters, Christian and Jordan, and a son, Brian.

Success Is Eminent If We Bond Together
DR. BARBARA WILLIAMS-SKINNER

"Thinking back to a time when I most had to remember my worth was around 1971-1972. I had attended UCLA Law School in the late 60s, early 70s, at a time women were not in top position anywhere; and the Women's Rights Movement had not yet become full blown," remembers Dr. Barbara Williams-Skinner.

In 1974, as a young woman she went to work as Executive Director for the Congressional Black Caucus (CBC) in Washington D.C., one of whose founding members was women's rights advocate Shirley Chisholm.

"Back then, you were often reminded that a woman's place wasn't in high lofty positions. You could be assaulted, insulted or marginalized at any time as the legal protection through sexual harassment laws had not been created. I got tired of being angry by the many times I was asked to get coffee in meetings by well intentioned people, or was approached inappropriately by men in high level leadership positions. It was a time of always having to prove one's self. The way you handled it made the difference. You had a choice to either be angry, or approach it from the standpoint of *don't get mad get smart*," she says.

The key to getting smart was to always be more prepared than anybody else. That meant before you went into any meeting, you should have done more research, rehearsed your talking points longer, and been clearer when speaking than anyone, male or female, in the room.

Success Is Eminent If We Bond Together

"The women around me then inspired me greatly, extraordinary women like Dr. Dorothy Height, who surely had gone through more than me. She was very active even pre-Civil Rights movement," says Dr. Williams-Skinner. In 1929, she was denied admission to Barnard College in New York because of her race. In 1963, she was not allowed to speak at the March on Washington merely because she was a black woman. "As both an African American and a woman, she was regularly victimized in a society that valued neither," she continues.

"I am grateful to have grown up at a time when you could touch and personally call on the role models around you. They were not too high, lofty or busy to provide invaluable mentoring and counseling, or just an encouraging word. The women around me taught me to *be ready at all times to stand up and be great. Nothing less than excellence would do. It was no one else's responsibility to educate you. You had to expect to do battle.* I was constantly reminded that *there were no excuses.*

In my day, I witnessed and was taught about women celebrating one another's success. It was a valuable gift to be able to be transparent. In doing so, we could learn from each other's success and failures. And we opened doors for one another. In 1994, I lost my husband and I was comforted through by having *sister strength - all the time.*"

"The sister-strength back then was strong. We banded together and were always in check with the ups and downs of one another's lives. African American women were marginalized to say the least, so none of us could afford to be loners."

"I remember an incident where banding together really opened doors. It was around 1996 when Bill Clinton was in office (elected 1992 and reelected 1996). There was a Cabinet vacancy at the Department of Labor and Sen. Edward Kennedy let it be known that he owned the right to pick the person to be nominated by President Clinton for that position. At the same time, Alexis Herman, who was Special Advisor to President Clinton, and former head of the Women's Bureau under President Jimmy Carter, also had her eye on a cabinet spot. She was interested in being Secretary of Labor, but was asked to consider the Secretary of Commerce spot given fact that Kennedy had a veteran from the labor movement in mind for Secretary of Labor.

One historical fact impacted Alexis Herman's decision to pursue the Secretary of Labor position. There had been an African American Secretary of Commerce, the late Ron Brown, in Clinton's first term. There had never been an African American Secretary of Labor. During her tenure as head of the Women's Bureau, Herman had focused heavily on getting women into non-traditional jobs. Becoming Secretary of Labor would seriously advance this vision.

When Alexis Herman decided to pursue the Secretary of Labor post, we knew we were in for the fight of our lives. We also knew there was a possible chance of winning, but only if we rallied women of all races and background to this cause. Dr. Dorothy Height led the charge by formulating organized committees of the top women leaders from all backgrounds from across the nation, including women's organizations, sororities, major African American organizations, and women faith leaders.

On May 1, 1997, when Alexis Herman was sworn in as the 23rd Secretary of Labor, everyone knew without ever saying it that we had prevailed over the nation's most powerful U.S. Senator. We did it through sister-strength and organization. Dr. Height regularly reminded us that 'success is eminent if we band together.' As women, we need to realize that *women make and bring a community together*. The best thing we can do to transform and unite our communities, and elevate the needs of women to the highest priority among our nation's leaders is to *never stop building strength and resiliency for a battle that never ends*," proudly declares Dr. Skinner-Williams.

MEET THIS WISE WOMAN OF COLOR:

Dr. Barbara Williams-Skinner is currently president of Skinner Leadership Institute, founded in 1992 by she and her late husband, evangelist, author, and pro sports chaplain, Tom Skinner. Skinner Leadership Institute works to provide leadership development, spiritual coaching, and bridge-building to groups as varied as Congressional leaders, Howard University college students, national clergy leaders, and young professionals.

Dr. Williams-Skinner is recognized in Presidential Who's Who Among Business and Professional Achievers (2008). She has served as Executive Director of the Congressional Black Caucus, and in 1981, she and her late husband, Tom, founded the Congressional Black Caucus Prayer Breakfast, which annually attracts thousands of faith and civic leaders from across the nation. Dr. Williams-Skinner has served on the boards of numerous organizations including the Dr. Martin Luther King, Jr. Center in Atlanta, Georgia, Volunteers of America, National Political Congress of Black Women, Operation Rainbow PUSH, Christian Evangelicals for Social

Action, Fuller Theological Seminary, and currently serves on the boards of Christian Community Development Association and Sojourner/Call to Renewal.

Dr. Williams-Skinner has written numerous articles including "The Power of Love," "Been There, Done That: Why African American Christians Resist Racial Reconciliation," "Why and How Would Jesus Vote," and "Obama, the Black Church, and the Promise of Reconciliation". She has also published two leadership training workbooks, Becoming An Effective 21st Century Leader and Personal Transformation Through Biblical Reconciliation. She is the mother of two adult daughters through marriage, 11 grandchildren, and seven (7) godchildren.

Dr. Williams-Skinner holds a Doctorate of Ministry and a Master of Divinity from Howard University School of Divinity, a Juris Doctorate and Master of Social Work from the University of California at Los Angeles, and a Bachelor of Arts from San Francisco State University.

Take the Leap and Believe
MAUREEN SIEH

Maureen grew up in Liberia where she was surrounded by relatives who were passionate about journalism and using the field to draw attention to social and economic injustices meted against the Liberian people by the government. One uncle edited a political magazine that was published in her grandmother's house where she lived in the 1970s. She began her journalism experience working on her high school newspaper. In high school, she also worked for the Daily Observer, an independent daily newspaper owned by her uncle Kenneth Best. The paper was the first independent newspaper published after the 1980 coup led by Samuel K. Doe, the young master sergeant and dictator who ruled Liberia for 10 years before he was killed in a bloody civil war in 1990.

"I was excited about journalism because I wanted to give voice to people who couldn't speak up for themselves. I was intrigued by the Daily Observer's fight for human rights." Maureen began working for the Daily Observer when she graduated from college in 1989.

She began her full-time career during a turbulent and challenging time in Liberia. On Christmas Eve, 1989, a civil war led by rebel leader Charles Taylor began in Liberia. Maureen became the first Liberian journalist to cover the war. She traveled to the battlefront and neighboring Ivory Coast and Guinea where thousands of Liberians had taken refuge.

"It was a scary time," and she couldn't believe she was there to witness and report on it.

"In the first two days of covering the war, I saw my Liberian people become refugees. I couldn't believe how things could change so fast."

During the height of the war, Maureen attended numerous press conferences where she questioned government officials, including President Samuel K. Doe, about the government's response to the war that was unfolding in her homeland.

At one news conference, Doe threatened to jail any journalist who reported about the war without the government's approval. It was another attempt to sanction coverage of the war. At the time, the Daily Observer was the only newspaper covering the war from the battlefront. Maureen interviewed government soldiers who had fled to a refugee camp in neighboring Guinea.

The government's threat about the war coverage prompted the Daily Observer to publish a blank front page the next day with an editorial explaining its decision. "It was scary, but needed to be done."

During Doe's 10-year reign, the newspaper was banned four times, its editors and reporters jailed numerous times, and burned down a few times for reporting on social and political injustices in Liberia. One of the burnings was for a story Maureen wrote about a woman whose husband was arrested and killed during the civil war. The newspaper's library and photo laboratory was destroyed, but that didn't deter the newspaper for continuing to cover the war.

Maureen left Liberia in May 1990 after she received a Fulbright Fellowship to pursue a master's degree in journalism. When she graduated two years later, she couldn't return home because Liberia was still at war.

She spent most of her career in America working for The Post-Standard in Syracuse, New York. She worked at the newspaper for 16 years where she made her mark covering underserved populations and ethnic communities. She wrote about refugees who started new lives in America and young girls having babies. "The more I wrote about urban communities, the more I wanted to empower women and young girls. I realized that was my calling," says Maureen.

Maureen had always thought about doing something else besides journalism, but didn't think she was quite ready to give up a career that had been a major part of her life. She got her chance to start something new when the newspaper offered a voluntary buyout. "If there ever was a chance to do something different, this was the time." She took the buyout in a time when the economy was hurting.

Maureen knew that if she wanted to change careers, she had to learn new skills. As a communicator, she knew she wanted to improve her language skills and get some experience doing international work. "Why not join the Peace Corps?"

That's when she realized her life was coming full circle, because her life was influenced by Peace Corps volunteers in her native Liberia. Her third-grade teacher and the vice principal of her Catholic high school were Peace Corps volunteers in Liberia. She knew that if they accepted her she "would be going to where it all started and giving back to America what it had given to her."

Maureen chose to use her waiting time to *chill* and she *trusted that God would give her what she really wanted or needed.*

After a year's wait, uncertainty of knowing if she was going, and where they would locate her; she was accepted. Peace Corps usually asks potential volunteers to indicate their country preference, but it's not always a sure thing. Maureen pushed for Morocco, because she wanted to improve her French and learn Arabic.

In September 2010, she left to Morocco and became one of the faces and voices of America in an Arab world. She started out teaching English, but soon began putting her journalistic skills to use. "I knew I wanted to share my journalism experience in some way," she said.

In her first year, Maureen wrote and received a grant to do a journalism workshop for Moroccan youth in Ouarzazate, the city where she works as a volunteer. With the support of the United States Embassy, the American-based Kids to Kids World Connect Program began. She organized a workshop for 55 youth teaching the basics of news reporting, writing, photography and how to use social media to give voice to their communities. Two young women who participated in the workshop were among 13 Moroccan women who participated in Global Girl Media, an international program sponsored by the U.S. State Department to encourage young women from disadvantaged communities to pursue journalism. After the workshop, about 25 participants organized a journalism club. The youth created a Facebook news page and have an Arabic and English online newspaper. Maureen also received another grant to do a multi-media workshop for the youth.

"My goal is to teach kids how to use video and photography to tell stories, so that they can work mostly in Arabic, the language that is widely spoken in Morocco. With the Facebook page and the online newspaper, we've been working mostly in English. When I leave, I want them to have enough journalistic skills to report in their own language."

She says that the entire experience has been a blessing. She has lived with wonderful Moroccan families and has enjoyed the cultural exchange, as well as the opportunity to learn a new language. "This whole experience has been a blessing. I'm glad that I had the opportunity to do something that I often hear people say, 'I've always wanted to be a Peace Corps volunteer.' Now, I can say, I've done it," and it's as rewarding as most people who have done it said it is.

MEET THIS WISE WOMAN OF COLOR:

Maureen Sieh is a former reporter and editor at The Post-Standard in Syracuse, New York. She resigned from the newspaper last August after working there for 16 years covering urban and ethnic communities. She had been reporting on the "Lost Boys" of Sudan since 2001.

In 2009, she traveled to southern Sudan on a World Affairs Journalism Fellowship administered by the International Center for Journalists.

The fellowship is sponsored by the Ethics and Excellence in Journalism Foundation. Maureen followed three former "Lost Boys" who returned to the villages they fled in 1987 to build schools, wells and clinics. Maureen began covering the "Lost Boys" since the U.S. offered to resettle them in 2000 because they had been living in a refugee camp in Kenya for 10 years.

Maureen is now serving as a Peace Corps volunteer in Morocco. The major focus of her two-year Peace Corps service is teaching Moroccan youth how to be journalists and use social media to give voice to their communities. The youth created a Facebook news page called Ouarzazate e-News and they also have an online newspaper in English and Arabic with the same name.

She Knew Who She Was
INDI L. SHELBY

She may have been the president of a non- profit organization, but she says that her professional role did not define her. She says it was clear that her family laid the foundation for her life from birth.

Indi had a very strong mother who became the backbone of her family. That's where she learned her values and perseverance. Her mom was a homemaker and took care of the entire family. Her father taught her that she could be anything that she chose to be if she truly believed in what she was doing. He was the provider of the home and they always lived in a house, because he worked to make sure of it. Even though her parents divorced when she was younger, they both were a very big part of her life. Her mom stayed with her for over 40 years so they were tight.

She says in her life she set many goals, which helped her to keep focused on a certain path. The highest credit goes to her faith, because it circulated around everything in her life. Both her aunts and her mother truly instilled keeping grounded and remaining faith-based no matter what she did. They said, "If you ever fall back rely on faith." That became critical.

If Indi had any struggle in her life it was the fact that she was different and she knew it. She was raised in New Jersey in a neighborhood where her family was the only integrated family on the block. It was like that for most of her early life. In high school and college there were never more than two minorities in the entire school. She graduated from Rutgers

University for both her undergraduate and graduate degrees. She was the first black student in their four-year nursing program and there were only two of them. Even so, she didn't experience out-and-out racism. She jokes and says that she must have been sheltered by her parents. There was one episode that she can recall that really alerted her to know that she was different. It was in college when a group of students called her out her name. She says, "You think you're one way then you find out differently." That's when she realized everybody didn't like her. There was another incident that was painful when she was in college and was invited to a classmate's wedding. She was excited and preparing to go with the other ladies only to get a call before the wedding to find out that the *place didn't accept blacks*. That made her take, many, many, steps back.

She began to ask herself, "What does this mean to me? What else will I have to deal with?" It was the 60s and racism did occur, she just hadn't really felt the sting until then.

Indi says that she wore braids and was all about Black Power. She remembers when she had one of her first jobs, she was told by her black female supervisor, that she couldn't wear her hair braided. "You can't represent the agency like that and besides it makes you look homely," she recalls her manager saying. Her response was, "What? This is who I am." She didn't take the criticism well and was offended hearing from *her*. She was hot and feeling like *you won't tell me anything*. It became interesting when one of her white colleagues pulled her aside to say, "Think about it. This is a company and they do have rules that we have to abide by." She went home, slept on it, and the next day returned to work with her braids in a neatly put-together bun. She had to learn to compromise. She was still proud of who she was, but she was also at work and had to be responsible to the job as an employee. "You can't always be so engaged in an idea or belief that does you or no one around you any good." She had to take herself out of the situation…and that became the turning point of her career.

Indi went from staff person to president of a company in her career; she says that it was influenced by faith. "I always believed that the Holy Spirit was there with me. Whenever I had to go into a meeting, do a presentation, or talk to staff, I would take a moment to breathe and say, *Thy will be done.* There was always a peace that would flow through me and I was open to allow the spirit to move. He was always there, and He never abandoned me. He gave me the right words and the right attitude."

"Knowing who I was carried me forward. It's not about your goals, being educated or anything. Unless you know who you are and who has you, then you'll never be successful," Indi shares.

MEET THIS WISE WOMAN OF COLOR:
In 2011, Indi L. Shelby retired from the Visiting Nurse Association of Central New York, Inc. after more than 24 years as director of patient services. For the past eight years, Ms. Shelby has served as president and chief executive officer of Visiting Nurses, A Systems, Inc. the parent of sister agencies, Independent Health Care Services, Inc., The Visiting Nurses Association Foundation of Central New York, and the Visiting Nurse Association of Central New York, Inc., as well as affiliate agency, CCH Home Care & Palliative Services, Inc. Her leadership has been instrumental in not only promoting positive change for all organizations

within the corporate system, but also for solidifying its position as one of Central New York's most trusted, respected, and widely known home care systems.

Her leadership style is focused on patient needs and service. Ms. Shelby believes that the most critical attributes of leadership are integrity and honesty with quality being her top priority, and she infuses her staff with this commitment.

Ms. Shelby's commitment and service transcends agency walls and into the community at large as evidenced by her dedication to and membership in many diverse organizations. She currently serves on the Board of Directors at Community General Hospital, Francis House, and the Home Care Association of New York State. Ms. Shelby is also a member of the Governor-appointed Home Health Care Reimbursement Workgroup, charged with studying the impact of changes to the home care reimbursement system.

Ms. Shelby earned both her bachelor's and master's degrees in nursing from Rutgers University.

7 Her Family Taught Her First
DR. AVIS A. JONES-DEWEEVER

Avis placed marriage very seriously in her life and wanted it to last. After all, while in college she started dating the person that she ended up marrying. She wanted the type of marriage that her parents had. They have been married for almost 50 years now and have a very good relationship.

It became clear that things in the relationship weren't right and over the years they weren't getting better. Ultimately, she made the decision to leave. She had children and didn't want her sons growing up believing that what they saw was what a marriage should look like.

She knew what she knew based on what she saw – a father that gave her great examples of what a husband should be like. Her dad was reliable, responsible, truthful, and loving; so she knew it was possible to have. She wanted her boys to witness that or nothing at all. She held true to her belief that an essential part of marriage is simply to be there; in the present, spending time and being part of a family unit. It didn't mean that her ex-husband was a bad person or father it simply meant she needed something different.

To this day, Avis supports the relationship between her children and their father. They love each other and he will always be their dad. She holds strongly to a belief, "No matter what happens between adults, you cheat the children when you don't allow and encourage that relationship (unless of course, there was abuse or something to that effect)."

Fortunate that her parents empowered her with confidence when she was growing up, she says it was not solely about them saying anything specifically about her potential or intelligence; instead, she really believed she gained a lot of strength from hearing their stories about what they went through and how they overcame their challenges.

She can recall several stories, but the ones that carried the most weight she happily shared in hopes to give a glimpse of life in her home. She says, "My parents had me when they were older – my mother was 40 – and they grew up during the Jim Crow South. They had to deal with what black people braved at that time. My mom grew up in the state of Virginia and school buses weren't provided to black children, only white children, so they had to walk several miles back and forth to school every day. Her parents along with other parents in the community, which was a rural community, pooled their money together, and bought a bus. The parents then took turns driving the bus to get their children to and from school."

Hearing stories like that made her grow up believing that she had the ability to be anything given the challenges her parents and grandparents overcame. "They did what had to be done and they didn't ask anybody for permission. They bucked the system and were very bold in their actions. So I always had within me that I'm not going to let anyone suppress me and make me feel that I'm less than."

The pride that they instilled in her, particularly relating to racial pride came through stories as well. Her grandmother was very influential to her.

Her Family Taught Her First

She says that she had a lot less time than she would have liked to with her because she passed away when she was in the fourth grade. Both of Avis' parents worked so her grandmother was basically her primary caregiver and they lived with her.

First of all, you had to know her grandmother. "She was a very bold person. She just said things and left you with no time to insinuate anything. You knew just where you stood about everything at all times. That's just how she was," Avis reflects. Her mom told her a story about how her uncle went somewhere, did something, and a white man said something to him that her grandmother didn't like. "So when she found out it was on. She couldn't drive or perhaps didn't even have a car at that time, so she walked all the way to this man's house, and cursed – him – out. My mom said that other people in the community were laughing because the man used to say no nigger ever cursed him, but he can't say that anymore! That's the type of person she was."

Avis says her grandmother was very light skinned and had green eyes. She will always believe that she was a product of white rape. She mentioned that only because she'll never forget an incident that happened at school. "It was the very first day of kindergarten and the first time I was surrounded by a number of white kids. I noticed that all the other black children in the class had brown eyes, but all the white kids had different colored eyes, you know blue, green eyes, etc. So, I came to this conclusion in my five year old mind that there it goes, my grandmother is white. So I came home and said, 'Oh grandma, you're white' – let's just say she was completely insulted and outraged and didn't speak to me for three days. That was the maddest she'd ever gotten at me."

At the time she didn't understand, but as an adult she understands a bit better says Avis. "Who knows what she saw in her life, but I say all that to say that all those instances made me feel, at least from a black perspective, that there's no reason to feel inferior. I am well versed in my history and I have never met anyone that made me feel as I was less than because of my race."

"At the end of the day, my family has always been really wonderful about making sure that their children know that you shouldn't let that stop you. We knew if a barrier came up the problem wasn't us. It isn't because of a personal deficiency; it's because of the ugly institutionalized reality of racism or separatism in our country. You have to do the best that you can to figure out your way through it," Avis states. One thing that bothers her is she's not sure if our women today are truly proud of who they are. Her role offers her an opportunity to engage with college students. "It really breaks my heart when I see young black women who have everything going for them, like brains, beauty, drive, ambition – everything and they say things that diminish who they are. Not only who they are now, but things to imply that they might want to dull their shine for the future because they think it might hurt their opportunities to find a mate." She spoke to a group where some wanted to go on to law school, but thought that if they did, they would have too much education and therefore, no man would want them. She couldn't believe what she was hearing.

Avis remembers, "My grandmother always told me 'God gives everybody a special set of talents and abilities that only you have. It's your responsibility to develop them and use them.' Just think you have this talent, ability and desire in your heart – that's your purpose."

"To think that you're willing to dull your purpose, put a cap on your purpose for some phantom of something you think exists is disheartening. Ultimately, even if you found a man that you think likes you because you are less than you could be, who is he loving? Is he loving the real you? Or does he love some muted version of you? How can that be successful? And what makes you think there is no partner for someone who is excelling? It would seem like the man that you want would be the man that will enhance your life and appreciate the fullness of you. Not someone who will be intimated by your success."

She says, "My father is the oldest son and he was 14 when his father died. So as the oldest son he's been working ever since to take care of his mother and his siblings. He ultimately became an entrepreneur, had a very successful business, and eventually employed all his brothers. So literally, he took care of his mother for the rest of her life, and by employing all his brothers he basically was taking care of all of their families all the way through retirement. All of that with just a grade school education. My mother is a college graduate and became a teacher. So there is that educational mismatch there, which is what these, young women were alluding to. I see how my father loves and respects my mother. He was not intimidated by her accomplishments, he celebrates them and she does the same for him. So I know that a real man will not be intimidated by a woman who fully develops her potential and will support her to be the best that she can be in all she does."

"I say all of this to say, I have no regrets about the decisions I've made in my life. Sometimes we have to close one door in order to open up a more promising future. I try to remember the lessons my family has shared with me and apply them to my life. I encourage our women to go use their God-given talents and abilities and always remember those who have come before them."

MEET THIS WISE WOMAN OF COLOR:

Avis A. Jones-DeWeever, Ph.D. is the executive director of the National Council of Negro Women. Both a membership and umbrella organization, the National Council galvanizes the collective power of more than 240 local sections along with 34 national Black women's organizations, which together represent four million women of African descent in the U.S. and throughout the Diaspora. An accomplished scholar, writer, and public speaker, Dr. Jones-DeWeever is an authority on race and gender in the American economy, poverty in urban communities, inequality of educational and economic opportunity, and issues of privilege, power, and policy in the U.S.

Milestones Look Different to Her
LISA ALFORD

Lisa grew up knowing that she could do many, many things. She grew up in an educated community, and had friends who were college and professionally oriented. She saw a large number of African Americans in different professions from being an ophthalmologist to being a professor. Even her dad retired as one of the assistant superintendents of schools in the school district where she grew up and her mom was a teacher; so education was very important to her.

She came from a family where both of her parents not only completed college, they each had graduate degrees. Lisa attended Hampton University for her undergraduate degree. It was there that her maternal grandmother attended many years prior. Her grandmother was granted a scholarship to attend what was then called Hampton Institute's (now Hampton University) pre-college program after graduating high school near the top of her class. Once the scholarship ended, lack of financial resources made it impossible for her to continue her studies. When Lisa graduated, she told her grandmother that she finished for the both of them.

It just so happens, that one of her life turning points came out of a challenge that occurred when she was completing her studies at Hampton.

When she was ready to apply to graduate school, she asked a professor at Hampton to be a reference; she knew she had good grades and there shouldn't be a problem. On one of the forms it asked for him to rank her among the top three to five percent of students he ever had. He told her that she didn't fit into that category. She was devastated.

She felt she had very good grades, even though she may not have scored as high on the standardized tests as others. That was a challenge for her to hear. She says that she was fortunate to have an emotional reserve and support of other professors and the head of the department, so that at the end of the day she didn't have to use him. But, she'll never forget the day before graduation. She saw the professor and he asked her what she was doing after graduation. He didn't know that she had received a fellowship from Ohio State to attend graduate school. She says she was so proud to say to him that she was going to Ohio State on a full-scholarship. His response was "Oh."

Lisa remembers another incident when she was student teaching. She had a vehicle so she was sent about 30-45 minutes away from the school. When she arrived she encountered a woman who was the student teacher supervisor who had such negative things to say about the students from Hampton, and she was not very quiet about it all. The woman spoke very highly about students from all the other universities that she had, but she couldn't find anything positive to say about them. So, Lisa went back to Hampton and told the head of the department how this lady just said horrible things about them and she wanted to know why he sent her there? He told her that he knew. She said, "You know? So why would you send me there?" He said, "Because I knew you could take it."

That fueled her and set her out to prove that woman wrong. She worked diligently to change her mindset of them. She says even in present day, she works really hard when people have no or low expectations of her. That incident carried over to and helped her to get where she is today.

There's a book called "Games Mother Never Taught You" that sticks in her mind. It talks about looking at people two levels above you and doing the things that they do. She often shares some of the lessons in her life that she's learned and gives advice on standing out. She'll let you know that she's comfortable being in situations where she may be the only person who looks like her. She says she's very comfortable striking up conversations with people she doesn't know; "You'll never know where your help is coming from and you will find that most people, if you ask them will help you."

Lisa enjoys being a help to her friends and she really likes quotes, sayings and scriptures. Her friends are always telling her *you have a scripture or quote for everything*. She grew up Baptist and keeps a Bible in her desk drawer. She says there are several times that she must refer to it to help her during the day with work related things, family related things, you name it. The biggest times in her life that she's had to rely on her faith comes to things related to her son, Caleb.

She had Caleb when she was 35. She was healthy and everything was expected to be normal up until she was about 22 weeks pregnant. That morning she went into the doctor's office under a little stress. She was in the middle of a federal review and had also received news that a close family friend had passed.

She realized something was happening, she found out that she was in preterm labor. She ended up being in the hospital for about a week and a half. She and her husband were hoping things would stabilize, and they seemed like they had. But then she started going into a more critical stage so they decided to do an emergency C-Section. Her baby was born at 24 weeks, which is very early. They told her he would have a very minimal chance of surviving. She was very devastated and even more so because she did everything as directed like take prenatal pills, yet the unforeseen still happened. She says, "There are some things in life that are beyond your control."

Caleb was diagnosed with autism and developmental delays, assumed to be because of his early birth. Many kids born autistic are born early. It has changed her life to only focus on what's most important.

She's learned to develop a positive outlook on things that we otherwise wouldn't believe to be good news. "Things that are insignificant to other people may be milestones in my world." She recounts how just the other day, Caleb was running from her, across the parking lot, and looking back like chase me. So she enjoys the moments that others may take for granted. She says, "People always ask me 'does he do this or do that' and there are many things he can do. I think the best thing about him is his laugh. It is so jovial that you can't help but laugh with him. For the things he is currently unable to do, I always say 'not yet'. We don't know what the future will be. The experience has helped me to appreciate life that much more and even in my workday, I'm able to provide a higher level of understanding to people and their needs."

Milestones Look Different to Her

MEET THIS WISE WOMAN OF COLOR:

Lisa Dunn Alford is the Onondaga County Commissioner of Aging and Youth and the President of Alpha Kappa Alpha Sorority, Inc., Iota Nu Omega Chapter in Syracuse, New York. She obtained a M.A. from The Ohio State University and a B.A. from Hampton University. She also received a Certificate of Advanced Studies from the Maxwell School of Citizenship and Public Affairs at Syracuse University in 2001 and from the University of California's Head Start Johnson and Johnson Management Fellows Program in 2005. Lisa has worked in various capacities in health and human services for almost 25 years working to ensure that those in need have access to programs and services that enhance their quality of life and strengthen the community.

Lisa volunteers with such organizations and groups as her church, sorority, her son's school, Junior League of Syracuse, Inc., League of Women Voters and other civic organizations. She serves on several boards and is the recipient of numerous honors and awards. Lisa believes in being her authentic self and sharing her gift of encouragement with others to inspire them to do the same. She strives to be consistent in her thoughts, words and deeds and sees every day as a fresh opportunity to honor herself, and those who blazed the trails before her. Lisa enjoys reading, public speaking and singing. Originally from Augusta, Georgia, she now resides in Manlius, New York with her husband and son.

One Blessing After Another
CARMEN DANIELS-JONES

It was 1986, she was 20 years old in college at Hampton University and her life was normal. During Thanksgiving break her life changed. She had a car accident and was paralyzed from the waist down. She went back to school in less than a year after the accident. "It seemed rather quickly I know, but I didn't know what else I would do with my life. I had nothing to lose and felt like what's the alternative if I don't go. Would I just live with my parents the rest of my life? While I love them and adore them that could not be my answer," she recalls, knowing that she had her whole life ahead of her.

She remembers exactly where she developed that attitude. She had a mentor in school who led one of the programs that she was involved with called Student Leaders. When the mentor learned that she was injured, she came over to the college and met with Carmen. "She was a tough-love type of black woman." At this time, Carmen was wearing a halo around her head, which was held by bars drilled into her skull. She came to visit about a week after the accident and while Carmen laid there in traction, she was pushing her to get back in school. She said to Carmen, "What are you going to do, stay with your mama and daddy all your life?"

So she went back to school. Her brother was a freshman as she was re-entering and that helped her to know she had support. She grew up in a Christian home and her family had faith and they were all praying for her to walk again. They clung heavily to word-faith theology, which she must admit could be destructive at times. "I'm not suggesting that God can't heal, but the desire others had for me to walk so badly would sometimes become a grand stand event. I had to hear God for myself about my own situation and that helped me to develop my own conviction. That took a number of years, but it helped me put a marker in the ground to say 'This is where I am, and who I am and I have to trust you God.' It was either what I learned and studied about God was true, or it wasn't." She chose to believe.

She says, during those intervening years, God really healed her heart and gave her a full life. She went back to school, dated, and got back into the social swing. Six years after the accident, she got married.

"When my husband Carlton and I began to have discussions about children, I grew very anxious. I wanted to start a family but was apprehensive because I was a paraplegic. But the Lord gave me a scripture from John 11:40, *Did I not tell that if you believed you would see the glory of God?* That verse leaped off the page and right into my heart. I started to write down in my Bible all the areas in my life that I did not believe. I needed assurance to be sure and I received that message. Within a short time after that, and with all the praying, I found out I was pregnant. I had my first child, a son named Marcus when I was 35."

Everything was going well in the pregnancy up until the seventh month. She required several sonograms due to her age and the disability, and that's when they discovered what looked like cleft lip.

The doctor performed amniocentesis to rule out a series of developmental issues and everything came back negative. She had a tougher time wrapping her brain around having a child with a defect than her husband. "We somehow marched on to our due date, July 11, 2001."

When Marcus was born, she was completely anesthetized and had a C-Section. When they delivered him he could not breathe. They soon discovered he had a very narrow trachea, which was smaller than a straw. "He was diagnosed with tracheal stenosis, and required a tracheostomy tube because he needed an open airway. Through the course of a year we discovered other health challenges that Marcus had, which centered around everything in the middle of his body. He was diagnosed with a condition called Opitz GBBB."

During the first year, Marcus probably went through 8-10 surgeries. She says it was a really hard road. They had a nurse in the house 24 hours a day. Their entire second floor became a nursing unit. They couldn't go anywhere because of all the equipment; "Nothing about our life was normal," says Carmen.

In the midst of that her husband was laid off from his job. "Thankfully, I had a job and we had good insurance, which was a huge relief because of Marcus' needs. We did all we could to stay afloat. I could clearly see how God redeemed my life after the accident, but I felt he was testing me again with Marcus."

"I always wanted children and in my heart wanted to adopt a child. After Marcus was born we were so entrenched in the world of having a disabled child that when things settled we decided to expand our family through adoption. In 2004, the family adopted Natalie, a journey that took only seven weeks from the time we got the application in, to the time we were told we had been selected as her parents. That was the best pregnancy of my life, Carmen offers with a smile."

Carmen shared, "As Marcus grew, many surgeries became elective, rather than urgent." By the time he was almost seven they decided to seek out attention to have his airway reconstructed. They were in the care of internationally renowned specialists at a children's hospital in Cincinnati. They were very excited about the surgery because it would get them closer to hearing Marcus' voice, as they had never heard him cry or speak.

The surgery was scheduled for August 2009. Before the surgery, they planned for Marcus and Natalie to spend a couple of weeks with her parents in Florida. Carmen was scheduled to fly to pick them up on July 3rd. However, the evening of July 2nd she got a call no parent ever wants to receive.

"Around 9 p.m. while dining with my friends, I received a call from my husband who was traveling in Africa. He told me that Marcus wasn't breathing and that they couldn't find a pulse. I screamed loudly in the restaurant and somehow drove directly to National Airport."

When she got there, she learned the last flight had left for the night. She subsequently called her pastor and he met her at the house. Her husband was in an airport alone in Senegal weeping and crying. He was supposed to be flying back that weekend to meet them in Atlanta. She remembers saying to him that Marcus would be fine. "We had emergencies before and we'd get through this." He sounded cautiously optimistic but reminded her that Marcus had never been without oxygen for such a long period of time before. He felt it was too long. "He shared with me that he called my parents at precisely the moment things were growing dire for Marcus. He ended up talking my dad through how to give our son CPR."

By the time she arrived at her house her pastor and girlfriends were there. They prayed. During that time Marcus was en route to the hospital. She was too emotionally wiped out to do anything and her girlfriends took care of it all – airplane tickets, packing her clothes, notifying her job, calling summer school to let them know Marcus would not be coming. You name it, they did it.

The next day her and a friend Robyn arrived at the hospital where her mother met them. Marcus was breathing on a vent and she met the doctor. "I could tell in his eyes that the news was not good. I was told the next three days would be critical. We began to pray, pray, pray. People all around the country were praying for our family," Carmen recollects.

While she was going to Tallahassee, her husband was flying to meet them from Senegal. Upon arriving and seeing Marcus, he almost collapsed. "We held on together and talked about our faith and rehashed John 11:40. Our whole family became coming in from all around the country, and our pastor flew from Washington, D.C. to be with us and hold a bedside vigil."

Within a few days it became clear that Marcus began shutting down. "Tests were run to see if there was brain activity…and there wasn't. We had to begin the agonizing process of saying goodbye. It was quite difficult to go from believing for a miracle and then shifting to preparing for him to be gone for eternity. That was such a difficult time – emotionally, spiritually, and psychologically. Carlton and I remained in his hospital room until he was wheeled down for surgery for his organ donation, realizing that this was the very last time we would see him this side of eternity." Marcus was three days from turning eight years old.

"While I had been involved in my own accident and emotional and spiritual recovery, losing Marcus was very different. I really needed God to lavish me with grace and strength. The only reason I knew I could get through it was because God met me after my accident. However, with the accident it was just me. This time I had to be strong enough for me and the whole family, and that included my parents. We are doing better. The journey of healing after losing a child is never done. The sting of the loss has shifted to a dull ache. Most days are fine, but once in a while a grief cloud will come. When it does, I pray for grace and strength to lavish us once again. I am sure that God isn't playing a game with our lives and that He is on our side. I know He is for me."

MEET THIS WISE WOMAN OF COLOR:

Carmen D. Jones is the Founder of Solutions Marketing Group and Senior Advisor to the US Department of Agriculture.

In 1986, Carmen Jones' life changed forever. While a student at Hampton University, Carmen and a group of friends were involved in a car accident during the Thanksgiving break. Carmen was severely injured, resulting in paralysis from the waist down. As a young woman who stood 5'10" she was unable to fully comprehend what life would be like in a wheelchair. Broken and without hope, Carmen was not sure what to do, where to turn, or how to respond. All she knew to do was to ask God to help her and that He did. How she went on to graduate from Hampton, get married, become a mother, and use her entrepreneurial skills to found a successful nationally-recognized business, and is now serving in the Obama Administration is an inspiration in itself.

In 2001, Jones' life took another unexpected turn and she gave birth to Marcus, a child with significant disabilities. During his first year, it was a day-to-day experience of wondering if he would live. Over the course of his life he underwent more than 20 surgeries. Carmen's life took yet another turn when Marcus passed away unexpectedly in July 2009. Carmen has had to face pain, grief, loss and great uncertainty. In the midst of it all, she has been sustained and encouraged by friends and family; and by developing an authentic relationship with God.

10 Always Keep the Faith and Believe
ELIZABETH (BETTY) MORROW

She grew up in Syracuse, New York, a small city of about 400,000 in Upstate, New York with her mother and sister. "My mother, Bessie Mitchell-Bowman, was very devoted to her church and community. I remember her as a church mother and a missionary where she often visited nursing homes, caring for the elderly members of the church who were sick. She also provided food for families and took new people arriving in the community into our home until they were able to find housing. Her faith and caring for others had a great affect on me. Around the age of 40, I had the feeling that I was put on earth to help others and to ease their pain and suffering."

After a failed marriage, Betty was left to care for her three children and she found a local church and became involved in many activities. She was mentored by the Pastor at the time and was appointed a local pastor at Hopps CME Church. She met her second husband at church and they both held offices until they decided to build a home in a nearby town. They continued to attend the church until a gasoline shortage caused them to join another church in their new town.

They became active in their new church and served on many committees. After several happy years, her husband, Samuel P. Morrow, was diagnosed with early Alzheimer's disease. "It was very stressful, the same as taking care of a child. I had to bathe him and cloth him. I remember a time when he began wandering at night. I would turn all the lights out and go to bed, then around 3:00 a.m. he would leave and go outside. I cared for him for nine years until the last months our doctor said he needed 24 hour care in a nursing home," she recalls. To help her get through the changes, she attended an Alzheimer's Support Group at her church and was chosen 'Caregiver of the Year' by the Onondaga County Department of Aging and Youth. This was in May 2002.

"Each time I left Sam at the nursing home, I cried all the way home. I kept thinking of the vows I had made in sickness and health. I would cry myself to sleep at night. Then I prayed and asked God to help me, because I had done all I could for my husband who now didn't know me," Betty remembers. "That night I slept and woke up the next morning with a feeling of peace and hope. I felt my faith had grown stronger and that I could go on. I felt like Job after he lost his family and his possessions, but still had faith in God."

In 1985, she lost her son to Juvenile Diabetes and a year later her mother to Parkinson's disease. "Now, my husband, Sam had a disease with no cure. He died on Valentine's Day, February 14, 2002. We were married for 31 years."

At church one Sunday morning, they sang 'Because He Lives.'
'Because He lives, I can face tomorrow
Because He lives, all fear is gone
And I know He holds the future
And life is worth the living just because He lives.'

"This song has given me a greater faith and purpose in life. As my ministry, I have started a group of older adults who attend a monthly luncheon at the church. We call ourselves OWLS (Older, Wiser, Livelier Souls). We number between 50-60 seniors, all ages 55-90+ and some cannot attend an early Sunday service, because of age and health problems. We meet each month in the afternoon and enjoy food, fun, and fellowship. God has blessed me in this ministry and has let me live to be 85-years-old and still trying to serve Him."

MEET THIS WISE WOMAN OF COLOR:

I am Elizabeth Morrow. I retired from the NY Telephone Company after 23 years. I have three children, nine grandchildren and nine great-grands I think; I quit counting after a while. I'm very active in the church, as an equalization member for the Central New York United Methodist Conference, and president and director of the OWLS. I was formerly co-facilitator of the Alzheimer's Support Group, chairperson of the Worship Committee for six years, president of the United Methodist Women, pastoral visitor at the Iroquois Nursing Home and a life member of the Telephone Pioneers. I live keeping the faith and believing, because God helped me to overcome my heartaches and made me stronger.

She Realized What Life Meant
LEVORE FREEMAN

Before being diagnosed with cancer, LeVore didn't realize what life truly meant and she couldn't imagine that she would face the disease again and again. Just a year prior, she had made a hard decision to quit her Fortune 500 job in order to attend nursing school full-time. At the time, she and her family were used to their lifestyle that two incomes provided and she knew that they would suffer but going back to school was her dream. Leaving her climb of the corporate ladder, LeVore found joy studying about what she really wanted to do. Then she learned that she had breast cancer. "I was sad and I wanted to see my kids grow up," she recalled. Thankfully with her husband's help, she was also able to finish school. While she studied, he watched the kids and took care of just about everything involving the house. "He is such a good man and has definitely been a blessing to me," she said, feeling like she never could have finished without him.

She dreamed of being a nurse early on, but it didn't quite work out after high school. Yes, she had cancer but it was the time for her to realize her dream and the goal was to graduate with her class. She would go to class then get chemo and after chemo, she went on to receive radiation treatments. LeVore served as an inspiration to many classmates, but she was uncomfortable with being put on a pedestal. She didn't feel like she was better than others; she just did what she had to do. She got through it and had 10 years of remission.

She Realized What Life Meant

Believing that she was done, she never thought the cancer would come back. So when it did, she remembers thinking, "Really, do I have to do this again?" She had to go forward. She decided to have surgery to remove both breasts and started chemotherapy again. LeVore fought through it. She says her pain hardly ever showed. There were few times where she had a moment, but she just got it out of her system and kept pushing through. The second time, the pain was more difficult but she endured.

The most devastating time was when cancer returned for a third time; it was now in her lung. She says, "I wanted to know why? What did I do wrong? I knew that God didn't do things to punish. That's not the way He is." Those were her quick thoughts. "All I can do is fight! I get tired, but deep down I know I can't stop. I must fight for myself and for my family. I don't know what God's plan is for me, but, I've accepted it better than my family. I am at peace, but I do wonder how it will affect them if I'm gone. My feeling is that I don't know when His plan is for me to die. I know I have to fight until God says it's time."

Currently, LeVore works on a hospital's oncology floor as a nurse navigator and she speaks to patients to explain what is going while giving them encouragement. When they are down, she shares her story with them. Once they hear about her personal experience with breast cancer, they are more willing to listen to her about surgery, radiation and chemo treatments. "I'm always willing to share my story. I feel it's important to hear people's stories so they know what to expect. It's helping put their mind at ease."

"I don't think I'm that different from others. I deal with trials the way they have to be dealt with – by putting all my faith in God. I believe in what He can do." She started sending text messages to her friends and family to keep them informed of how she was doing. She doesn't know when but she eventually started sending scriptures and she doesn't know why; it just happened. Now she sends out daily inspirational messages hoping that people will hear them and getting something good out of what she's doing. The words touch and she gets responses from family, friends, and people from work saying that she reminds them of how to feel; others draw strength from her messages. The days she's not feeling well, LeVore sends out prayer requests. That's when she receives responses that build her up, giving her strength. When she starts feeling sorry for herself, she will usually hear a story of someone that is facing something worse and it will make her snap out of it.

LeVore also enjoys reading and studying the Bible. She didn't study it until later in life, but loves when she's reading God's message and his love for us. She also enjoys the messages she receives by reading daily inspirations. She says there is always so much to learn, "My faith is strong. I trust Him with my life because He is merciful. I am a sinner, as we all are, but He still loves me. He'll always be there for me. When I feel bad, He always helps me get through."

LeVore asks that if you take something from this story, let it be a lesson on our strength:

"We always emphasize that we are supposed to be strong black women, but we must also realize that we need to be able to express our feelings without feeling weak and ask for help when we need it. When it is that

point in time when things are really hard, tell your family/friends how you really feel. Sometimes I need to know that I can turn to my sister or friend and just let it out. Some days I don't want to be strong, I want someone to listen to me. Just Listen. Listen to how I feel. Allow me to have a day of venting. Don't let me stay down, but don't make me feel guilty that I'm having a bad day. Encourage me by praying with me and for me."

Another lesson is to listen to your body. She found her own cancer every time. She knew her body and when she didn't feel right, she had it checked out. "So many black women are diagnosed with cancer at a late stage. Many could have received treatment that could have saved their lives. We have to be willing to look out for ourselves and even though it is scary, you should never ignore your symptoms. It's not going to go away. I'm not saying it will always work out, but you want the best chance you can get. I am thankful that I have been able to be treated and I will continue this fight with God on my side," she declares.

MEET THIS WISE WOMAN OF COLOR:

Fighting breast cancer has become a major part of my life, but it does not define me. I have a very loving husband that I adore and who has been with me every part of this journey – my rock. I have two wonderful children that I love and adore and have also been blessed me with two beautiful grandchildren. After having a successful business career, I realized that I was not following my lifelong dream. After much contemplation, I was able to quit my job and go back to school for nursing. I fulfilled my dream of becoming a nurse at the age of 39, even after being diagnosed with breast cancer in my second year of study. Being an oncology/bone marrow nurse, and recently oncology nurse navigator has brought such fulfillment to my life. I love taking care of my patients and letting them know that I know exactly what they are going through because I've been there. I'm often asked if I became an oncology nurse because of my experience, but I honestly decided this field before being diagnosed. I was cancer free for 10 years and unfortunately it came back in 2008. I'm still fighting!

Through my journey with cancer, people have always told me how strong I am. I guess I am strong but I just look at it as doing what I have to do to get through. It's been tough, but I draw my strength from my Lord and Savior. He has always been with me, even when I did not realize it, and lifts me up when I need it – and that has been quite a bit. I give Him all my thanks and praise. Texting my family/friends of how I was doing has now morphed into a daily text of scripture. I love the responses I get back from time to time, letting me know how it has affected them. I know I have a purpose and that God has a plan for me. I'm just trying to follow along.
~ LeVore

12 She Had to Go Through It to Get Through It
PAT OSBORNE

"The greatest testimony I have is surrounded by the fact that I was raped. Not saying that it was a good thing that happened to me, but it turned me around, changed my life, woke me up and now I'm able to share that experience with someone else or other people who have suffered that same abuse and help them come to grips with it," Pat shares.

In this case, she felt like she brought it on herself in some respect. She says she was living a fast life. At the time, she was divorced, not receiving child support, had no job and convinced herself that making quick money was just a temporary means of survival. "I was the only woman in the game in that area; so I felt a bit of prestige, running with the big dogs."

"Some men broke in my house intending to rob me, but since I was there, you know – I don't dwell on that night but I'll never forget it. My daughter must have been around 11, and I was about 30. I'm 57 now. She was watching TV in my room and we both drifted off to sleep. When I woke up there was a shotgun next to my head and there were three other guys ransacking my room. They pulled me out of my room and raped me in my daughter's room. She slept through the entire ordeal. As insane as it may sound, I knew it was God…it was an awakening… a sign for ME! My daughter was protected by the grace of God. I got up with my share of bruises but alive and changed. The following Sunday I started attending church because I was so thankful that He opened my eyes and kept hers closed. That was it."

She remembers when the police came in to complete their report; they were in disbelief. They thought she knew the people because she was so calm and relaxed. "Hey, it was over. I was so grateful that it was no worse than it was. I wasn't dead, they didn't touch my daughter, nor did she awaken to witness anything. What happened to me didn't even matter. At the time, she was my only child and my only concern."

To date, she hasn't been involved in any rape crisis units or organizations established directly to help other rape victims, but friends who know her story have asked her to speak to other women who have also gone through it to help them move pass it.

"For me, my healing process began by taking accountability for my actions. It wasn't like someone grabbed me off the street. My actions placed both me and my daughter in danger, so just waking up and realizing how it could have been so much worse was my turning point. If they had raped her I would have probably gone totally insane. So the fact that she was protected was a message from the Universe to me saying, 'Get your act together.'"

Pat doesn't compartmentalize herself by limiting her beliefs about God. She considers herself spiritual saying, "Religion is for people who are seeking God, and spirituality is for people who have found God."

"Acknowledging the consequences of your actions (karma) when it rolls around is one of the key components of wisdom. They could have killed me and the honest truth is I could have gotten myself and my daughter killed. The key is to go through the experience (whatever it is) but don't miss the lesson. As my girlfriend says, 'It ain't nothing but something.' That horrible invasion of my home and my body actually strengthened me. Instead of falling apart because I was raped. I was rejoicing that I was still breathing and wise enough to know that God had given me another chance to become the woman I am destined to be. As long as I wake up another day, with an outlook for a happier life, I leave all of that negativity behind me. That was yesterday's news."

That's her testimony. If anybody asks her what changed her life, she says, "I openly tell them what happened to me and how I overcame it. I didn't let it break me. I'm stronger than that."

She wants to say to women, "Instead of focusing on what happened, focus on what didn't happen. God gave you the ability so that you can handle it! I am so thankful, so thankful."

MEET THIS WISE WOMAN OF COLOR:

One of my greatest assets is my ability to find something positive (and sometimes even humorous) in even the most negative circumstances. For example I'm not a 50 something year old woman – I'm $39.95 plus shipping and handling. I haven't had a series of unsuccessful marriages/relationships – they were successful practice runs for the man who will become my lover, friend and inspiration to grow as an individual, as well as his companion. Following those practice runs, I raised my heartstrings (my daughter and son, ages 39 and 24 respectively) as a single parent, and I often apologize to my mother for what I must have put her through. My job description is to love life, spread joy and share wisdom – working as a project manager is just how I pay the bills. I'm intelligent enough to know tomatoes and cucumbers are fruits and wise enough not to put them in a fruit salad.

Over the years I've learned to distinguish between guilt and responsibility and the importance of setting boundaries and learning to say NO. I've stopped allowing people to be my priority, while I'm just their option. And, I finally discovered I deserve to be treated with love, kindness, sensitivity and respect – and I won't settle for anything less.

For me happiness is having something worthwhile to do (purpose); someone to cherish (love); and something in which I hope for (vision/faith). I believe God has already placed whatever it takes to make us better and happy within our reach...it's up to us to figure out what it is.

Inhale peace... exhale love... be inspired.

~ Pat

13 A Dollar Bill Isn't Enough
KITRA WILLIAMS

It was 1980, her last year of college when she realized she had some acting ability. After graduating from Cheyney University having received her B.A. degree in music education with a concentration in opera, she knew there was more awaiting her. Once she accomplished the goal of representing her college as homecoming queen, she began to recognize her talents and abilities. She began studying under the direction of the famous kid star Todd Bridges' mother, Betty Bridges. That would eventually lead her into auditioning for the role that landed her first "leading lady" opportunity starring for the gospel musical icon, Michael Matthews. He was affectionately known in the gospel playwright industry as "The Godfather of Gospel Musicals." He paved the way for many upcoming directors, actors and playwrights like her and even greats such as Tyler Perry, David E. Talbert and many others.

The opportunity to have worked with such phenomenal directors allowed her to prepare for even greater works. It mainly helped her to have confidence in herself. Her faith allowed her to believe in the gifts God had invested in her despite that she often had slow and sometimes no phone calls.

She would later land the leading roles in Tyler Perry's "Diary of a Mad Black Woman," Bishop T.D. Jakes' "Woman Thou Art Loosed" and Oprah Winfrey's Broadway Musical, "The Color Purple." She says starring with Fantasia was the best. She realized through her directors just how blessed she was. The experiences also prepared her with the opportunity to explore and express her talent through some of the greatest challenges she would later encounter.

She knew that she was different and believed that's what got her many favorable positions and opportunities. But it also caused her great grief and left her often just trying to fit in. She was known for telling a story and not just acting. She says it was a very precarious situation while desperately trying not to stick out like a sore thumb.

So, in waiting between the five-year gap and even years later, she began finding herself. It was exciting because she never saw greater things for her life NOT happening. She always knew and believed that God was going to do something special in his perfect timing. But while waiting, she had some unbearable challenges in fact; it was one period in time where both she and her son actually became homeless. It was about a two-week span where she got into an argument with a new apartment manager. The manager wanted her to get rid of her dog or pay extra to have him there. She gave her an ultimatum and after seven years of residency there, Kitra packed up their things and headed for the car. Kitra says, "I'm called a woman of radical faith. Because when God tells me to step out on the water, I'll step out on the water… and after I've stepped out on the water, I step out on air."

As a single parent and industry girl, miracles followed her all of her life. She remembers during the time of homelessness, she was driving in her car when she got a call from an old friend that she hadn't heard from in years. She told her she needed to get her son to an audition in Hollywood. Her

A Dollar Bill Isn't Enough

son, Jarah was about nine years old then and they were looking for a kid to throw a basketball in the basket for a Nestle commercial. They got there and the casting team fell in love with him. They asked for her number and at the time all she had was a cell, which was about to be turned off. She told them, if this number gets cut off, dial her 800 number. It had not yet connected, but it was free and a friend told her about it. She knew it would be on within 24hrs of ordering it but because of personal hardship she was too distracted to even check the messages. The woman called her back two days later and she said, "Where are you? We tried to call you. We selected him! It was a 100,000 deal where were you?" She said, "Lord please don't tell me that!" The woman replied, "I'm sorry but they gave it to another kid and I just hate this."

She just broke down and cried. She shared with the woman her situation telling her how they really did need that job. How they had lived in this place for almost 8 years etc. The woman said, "You know what? The minute I first laid eyes on you I felt a kindred spirit." She said, "Why don't you come stay with me and my husband?" They had a beautiful five-story home and just had the basement crafted by Disney. She said, "It's been made into a dungeon and your son will absolutely love it." She asked her, "Would you come live with us? You take care of me, and I'll take care of you." The woman eventually ended up giving Kitra money for a better car and her own place for her and her son…" My God will take you further than any dollar bill!"

Psalm 23:6 is one of Kitra's favorite Scriptures. *Surely goodness and mercy shall follow me all the days of my life.* She has found when there is a special anointing upon your life the enemy will violently chase you, but she's reminded through the word of God that he will first have to get through goodness and mercy before he can get to you. She says, "That will NEVER happen!"

The role in "Woman Thou Art Loosed" was another blessed and favorable opportunity for her. Tyler called her up one day and said, "You don't know me but I've heard your anointed voice and a director I inquired to about you would not give me your contact information but I got a little birdie to give me your number and we want you to have the leading role of 'Woman Thou Art Loosed' with top billing." Of course, she screamed YES! That was the beginning of great financial reestablishment for her. Bishop T.D. Jakes took care of her well.

She cannot share her story without mentioning the greatest man who has ever come into her life, "Dr. Bobby Jones of The Word Network. The favors and grace working through that man in my life even until now is immeasurable. Doc. I love you, you are the best! You, Jesus, and my darling son, Jarah, helped me keep it together. Thank you!"

She really felt like she had *arrived* when she'd received the physical manifestation of being on Broadway doing "The Color Purple." It was a confirmation of a prophetic word she received from God years prior. That was the epitome of her career.

You can also find her hand to the plow on the silver screen playing the role of Mama" in "Roscoe's House of Chicken n Waffles". It's in Blockbuster stores worldwide. And although she's shared the privilege she still believes the big screen has far more to offer, awaiting her greatest element.

A Dollar Bill Isn't Enough

Last but not least, you can find some of her greater works encouraging the nation's youth during her Million Youth Peace March International on Capitol Hill. She has a special love for the youth and their social and economic concerns. It is her desire to show single parents that they can raise children with morals and values that will impact their lives in a greater way. "To teach them that true success no matter how long you must wait on it, it comes from God. And, to never give up on you," she imparts.

Kitra believes, "In lieu of the many roles I've played and opportunities I've had, I can't think of one greater than sharing my untold story."

MEET THIS WISE WOMAN OF COLOR:

Singing phenomenon and actress, Kitra Williams, was voted outstanding in her renown leading role performances of T. D. Jakes' stage play, "Woman, Thou Art Loosed" and Oprah Winfrey's Broadway Musical "The Color Purple".

Kitra is founder of The Agape Academy and Agape Theater and Film Awards, which honors underprivileged multi-culture youth, through the art of family based film, theater and cartoon animation.

Kitra is ecstatic about her latest mandate as chair -organizer for America's first Million Youth Peace March The anthem she wrote for President Obama's Inauguration entitled, "A New Birth of Freedom" was recently sung as the opening song for the Washington, D.C. Fourth of July parade and will be nationally released and sung with a thousand-voice choir during the Million Youth Peace March. Listen out for Kitra.

14   **Doing a Praise Dance**
REKISHA ARI SQUIRES

She moved to the Washington, D.C. area around the age of 25 to attend college and get a degree. She had come from Sacramento, California where she grew up with a rough, fast way of living. Her dream was to be an entrepreneur, work for herself, and have her own.

Rekisha says her ambition got the best of her after she graduated from college. Her mom passed away shortly thereafter, and she received an inheritance. She used the money and invested in a business. Of all things, it was a dance studio. "I opened it in 2005 based on a need in my community. I lived in a suburban area where there were several dance schools, but none of them catered to minorities. It was quite visible to see that our kids weren't in the dance schools. The studios would have about 200 students with two or three of us. At the end of the day, they just didn't market to us, so that's why even though I'm not a dancer I decided to put something out there."

"You can say I have always been an entrepreneur at heart. I've tried everything from the network marketing businesses to you name it. I was quite ambitious, and I never knew what it would be like, but now – I'm walking in it," says Rekisha.

So, she started the business and was faced with several setbacks going in blindly. She didn't have the proper research nor a plan. In 2007, when the economy flopped, she lost everything that she had invested and earned. She would pay out till the last dime moving her business to several different locations. "I felt like giving up so many times."

But like she said, she's always been that entrepreneur at heart and she always had the faith that this is what she was destined to do. She had seen the kids and saw how much joy they had when going to class to perform; being around other kids and teachers that looked like them. That kept her going. "That's how I knew I was on the right path, doing the right thing," Rekisha shares.

She says it may have seemed like she was crazy for investing everything in her business, but at the end of the day she felt she was doing something for her community. She just knew it was the right thing to do. She saw the vision, but it just wasn't in her control. "I had to listen to my spirit and let it guide me."

"So I went through the times of being broke. Sometimes I had $5 to my name and just didn't know what to do. One day, I just received a blessing. God just brought people to me right when I was at the edge. He sent me people and I was able to start over. I learned my lessons from going in blind, so this time I actually did a business plan."

She had a corporate job before, but now she was making triple. She started reaching more children and doing more things geared toward giving back to the community. "So I always encourage people to never give up. You never know if the next day could be your breakthrough. You have to walk in faith and just know that you will get there."

"If I had to tell you anything else I would say surround yourself with good mentors. I am thankful for the many mentors in my life, especially my mom. She was my backbone and my mentor. She used to tell me many stories about her struggles as a school psychologist. I saw her remain strong as she would talk about racism that she always went through. But, she always kept her head up. She taught me that you will have your setbacks and your struggles, but that's just life."

MEET THIS WISE WOMAN OF COLOR:

Rekisha Ari Squires, a native of Sacramento, California is a dedicated wife, and mother, who tirelessly serves her community. After graduating from Howard University, Mrs. Squires placed Ari's House of Dance & Performing Arts Studio into action after discovering the lack of diversity in the performing arts schools in Stafford and Fredericksburg, Virginia, where she now resides. After an unsuccessful search for a dance school for her daughter that offered authentic hip hop dance classes and ethnic dance teachers who catered to a multi-cultural community, Ari discovered quickly that she had work to do. Through hard work, dedication and a whole lot of prayer came the birth of her dance school to the city of Stafford in 2006. Since the arrival of her studio, Ari has developed professional dance teams that have won record-breaking awards and have been featured in a national television commercial. She has also founded Lend-a-Hand, Uplift-a-Child Foundation, a non-profit organization providing mentoring and leadership programs for teens, hosting "Pretty Girls Rock" symposiums and "Boys to MEN" impact and discussion forums for young girls and boys.

Doing a Praise Dance

Her ultimate goal is seeing smiles on the faces of young men and women who might ordinarily not have a reason to smile. Ari has mastered the term "pay it forward" understanding that someone, too, helped to mentor and pave the way for her success. Giving back to those that have been disproportionately served is what gives her the most joy. Not too often will you find business owners more concerned with helping the needy than the mighty dollar. She understands that what you give to the youth...you get back in your senior years, because these are the children of our future.

15 Know It Then Focus On It
RHODA ROJAS

Being laid-off made her realize how much she placed her value and dependence on her job. To her, this was a big part of how she assessed her worth. Her breakthrough came in her downtime as she searched for an understanding of herself. She says that she understood that she was "living in the motion" and she had to "strive to continue building her relationship with God."

In search of guidance she began looking for a church home and started attending bible study. It was there, that Rhoda says, "At different points in life, we all stumble and crawl before we walk again. I had to choose to enjoy every journey, and I learned that regardless of where it may take you be humble instead of being angry, because no result will come of it. A humble attitude will allow you to see your full potential, and others will see areas for you to develop." This emotional and spiritual journey led Rhoda to live her life to the fullest and during her transition she found a new focus that rechanneled her energy.

This single woman, who has no children, found figure competing as a way to stay active. She didn't get into it for the look of it. She got into it, because she enjoys a good challenge. This was something that was different for her and it would allow her to do things she takes pleasure in like strength training and cardio; most of all it requires a commitment.

Know It Then Focus On It

She says that people ask her all the time about competing, but more importantly they want to know how they can lose weight. She tells them to set a challenge. She first tries to assess what they are trying to do, because if their only goal is to lose 5-10lbs, then this is not the route they want to take. She tells people that they have to look at what's going to make them want to fundamentally make changes in their lives. When she ventured into this realm she had to change her eating habits and even change how and when she hung out with friends. This was no easy task, it was a three-month commitment and she lived in the gym. Her social life basically halted during that time due to the strict training regimen and she says, people didn't get that and she lost friends. It's a decision.

She says that timing is also important. When she was just going through the motions of life, she woke up, went to work, came home, and if she worked out she did, if she didn't then she didn't. She knew that she was bored and she really wanted to do something different and meaningful.

Rhoda says that she was introduced to competing through someone that she barely knew who had competed before. She was intrigued by the woman's workout and asked questions about her training. Without hesitation the woman shared her trainer's information. It all happened suddenly, and before Rhoda knew it she had set up an appointment with the trainer. That was in January 2009.

She met with the trainer and that was the beginning of her journey to get in shape. It also extended her interest in possibly competing in a show one day. When she asked the trainer about it, she was told, "I don't know if you'll be ready to be in a show yet, but we'll see how you progress, and see how you do with getting ready, and if you are ready for a show then we'll determine that then." Three months later, the trainer said, "You can do the show." Rhoda was surprised and that became the part of her wow experience! She was thinking I'm actually going to be on stage.

During her journey she lost weight and became more fit. She now recommends people to take pictures before and after. She didn't and wishes that she had. She says, "It helps you to see where you came from and pictures speak louder than words. You remember those memories." She got to the point where she lost a lot of weight but she still didn't see it; at least, not until the competition.

She was 34, and for the first time she realized that she had a total body transformation. She had muscle and she felt good about herself. Back then training helped her to think about something else other than worrying about finding a job. Now, working out is part of her everyday life. She says, "It keeps me mentally and physically healthy."

Rhoda says that if nothing else it has helped her to lay a good foundation for healthy living. Her mindset has even changed in regards to the possibilities of her body figure after she has children. She knows now that she can do anything if she focuses on it.

Rhoda finds that in competing she is able to motivate others. She is realizing more and more the importance of helping others in this realm and understands that there is more to her purpose to uncover. She is excited about her continuing journey and prays that she is able to take the leap of faith to do what God has in store for her next.

~ /// ~

When it comes to fear, she says, "You just gotta do it! There is nothing to fear, but fear itself. It sounds easy, but it's the truth. It's part of the journey and this is who you are, period! If you want people to see you and know you for who you really are say to yourself, I truly can do this as well." She believes that "You have to live life as if every day is an event. When you live your life that way you tend to really enjoy it no matter what day it is."

MEET THIS WISE WOMAN OF COLOR:

I was born and raised in St. Croix U.S. Virgin Islands. When I graduated from high school I moved to Washington, D.C. to attend The George Washington University. My first year at GW, I was studying to become a veterinarian, because I love animals. I quickly learned I did not love learning all the infinite information on cells and chemistry and how they work. I still love animals but found my strength in the business world. I graduated with a degree in Human Resources and currently am a Human Resources Business Partner with McKesson.

Living in D.C. I started salsa dancing, which I still do today and my goal is to do a performance in the Atlanta area with a salsa troop. I also trained and completed the Marine Corp Marathon in 2000.

After seven years in D.C. I moved to Orlando, Denver, New York and back to Denver in 2003. While living in Denver I ran two half-marathons and two 10Ks. I like running but since it was not my passion I turned to another sport, figure competitions. In 2009 I competed in my first show and placed 5th in the Colorado state competition. I have completed four shows total and this year I hope to make it my best.
~ Rhoda

Still Learning to Be the Best Her
KEIWANA MCKINNEY

Keiwana shares, "My journey began when I decided to shut down my braiding salon and continue my education. I knew it would take me at least seven years to surpass what I had accomplished at the height of my status as an entrepreneur. The decision to close my business came easy because I had built a house of straw."

When she was in the tenth grade, most of her friends had already graduated from high school. In a one-year period, she left high school, secured a GED, and attended the University of the Arts. In her computer graphics course, she had a revelation that sparked her entrepreneur spirit. "As a person who wore hair braids, I understood the investment. My goal was to have a braiding salon that offered digital consultations. I opened a salon and learned the difference between a businessperson and a person in business," she states.

"My accountant sent me to Wharton's Small Business Development Center to bring me face-to-face with my lack of business acumen. I was exposed to the University of Pennsylvania's campus and the brilliant minds of professors who worked in the Small Business Development Center." After she attended the sessions, she realized that she was not passionate about her business. "Yet, I was an excellent hair braiding consultant who developed a profitable public relations campaign that brought in more money than a neophyte could have imagined." Her time at the Small

Still Learning to Be the Best Her

Business Development Center required her to critically think about the direction she wanted the business to go in, and what she was willing to sacrifice in order to make it happen. "I concluded that money was good, but not everything. What I needed was to continue my education, so that I could make the big bucks."

Once the business closed, the next order of business was to put an end to a negative personal relationship that went from good to bad. In the beginning, it was a loving relationship between two young people from disadvantaged communities who found strength in each other's ambition and companionship. "As we matured, the relationship became unhealthy and gratitude turned into resentment. In short, there are talkers and there are doers. I was able to develop a plan to pursue my dreams, and he was only able to dream. This led to a collage of unwarranted abuse that required me to develop an exit strategy out of the relationship."

She found peace at the home of her best friend, Denise, who lived about a mile away from Langley Air Force Base. She had recently retired from the United States Air Force and was a friend that could be depended on. Twenty-two days later, she left Virginia to return to Philadelphia. Denise tried to convince her to stay a little longer, but she told her it was time for her to go. "I felt it in the wind that it was time to spread my wings and to play out the new chapter in my life," Keiwana says.

"During this time my faith was unwavering. I strongly believed that when things got really bad, there was a message in that bad. For me, bad times were the right time to look in the mirror. In my mind, I was being called to exhibit the faith that I proclaimed to have when times were good. When the rubber met the road, I found my true value in the clarity that I was given by the grace of God. My inner voice told me *this is my tragedy, but I will learn a lesson that makes me the woman I am destined to become.* I moved forward patiently and built my house of brick."

When she started school at the Community College of Philadelphia, it was a new start. Before she enrolled, she took a career interest test (CIT) that helped her to identify what career was best suited to fit her personal interest. She decided to pursue a degree in communications and became active in the student newspaper, as well as student government. The CIT taught her what student activities to get involved in and how to solicit letters of recommendation for internships that could serve as a bridge to her career. She landed two internships; one at TV3 and the other at the City of Philadelphia Commerce Department.

"I always remembered what Wharton SBDC taught me, which was to stick with your passion. When I read Oprah Winfrey's unauthorized biography, I learned an important lesson about trying to force yourself to do what doesn't work for you. Winfrey was a communications major. After she experienced success as a radio host, she seized an opportunity to leave her hometown and become a news anchor. This turned out to be a disaster because Winfrey was uncomfortable with reading from a teleprompter. As things went from bad to worse, the station decided to use Winfrey as a host for their morning show. Needless to say, she was a success and eventually grew to become the Oprah that we all know. As a former entrepreneur, I found the most pleasure in my internship with the commerce department, because I helped business owners cut through the red tape when doing business with city agencies and departments. Therefore, after I graduated

Still Learning to Be the Best Her

I said bye-bye to the glamour of TV3 and stuck with my passion," she recollects.

She became a representative for the Mayor's Business Action Team, a division of the Philadelphia Commerce Department. A year later she informed her boss that she decided to continue her education and would be moving on. A farewell celebration was held in her honor, and the director of the commerce department presented her with a Liberty Bell from the Mayor of Philadelphia. She received many gifts and well wishes.

Shortly after leaving her job she gave birth to Galaxy Enterprise (Galaxy), which was a private-business consultancy. Galaxy was contracted by the Street Campaign to develop a plan that galvanized voters between the ages of 18-35. After many trials and tribulations, that campaign came to an end and Keiwana says, "I experienced a personal victory when the Mayor gave his victory speech. His opening words were 'You had to be at Broad & Olney!' This was a reference to an event that was organized by Galaxy. In Philadelphia, a major transportation hub is located at the corner of Broad and Olney. On Election Day, during the peak hours of 5 to 6 p.m., I scheduled to have the Mayor at this location to take Polaroid pictures with his constituents. This was instant gratification for all parties involved. There was a multimedia truck with big flat screens that showed videos of the Mayor and played music produced by Philly International to promote the campaign. Members of Galaxy's street team greeted constituents and blanketed the area with campaign paraphernalia. The Mayor was so excited that we did the same event the next day, but this time it was filmed. Next, Galaxy received a sub-contract to organize the Mayor's Neighborhood Inaugural Ball. These opportunities did not pay well, but they exposed Galaxy to the city's movers and shakers and earned the company a reputation as one that delivered."

By the year 2006, the company had reached a point were $40,000 was made in less than six days. "I knew then, if I put my mind to it and continued to work with integrity, the sky would be the limit. I made money, but I was tired. Everything that I did required me to physically be present, so I wondered how I could make money in my sleep.   This has become my next quest, says Keiwana.

MEET THIS WISE WOMAN OF COLOR:

At the age of five-years old, my father taught me there is no such thing as a no win scenario. To anyone who finds inspiration in my story, know that I learned from the several failures that came before each win. The wisdom of my father's words is what gave me the courage: to accept and learn what I could have done differently when things didn't go my way; to stand, after the fall, with my feet planted in the dignity of my good intentions; and to never give anyone, or anything, the power to deter me from the pursuit of my dreams. My father is not a rich man and he never lived a virtuous life. However, he gave me the words that ensured I check my ego at the door in the face of defeat and know that what is for me is for me.

To date, I am a non-traditional student at the University of Pennsylvania in pursuit of a Doctorate degree in Critical Cultural Communications. My experience at the university has been rewarding, enlightening, and robust. I will forever be grateful to my mentor and friend, Dr. Therese Flaherty, professor at the Wharton School of Business. She inspired me to continue my education and explore all that life has to offer.

Still Learning to Be the Best Her

Prior to becoming a student, I engaged in political activities that positioned Galaxy for growth. My godmother, Joann Bell, provided me with the platform needed to showcase my skills and receive notable contracts as an upcoming businesswoman. Willie F. Johnson, mentor, and friend, introduced me to members of the business community that supported Galaxy's philanthropic activities. As a result, I was able to touch the lives of thousands of people in the City of Philadelphia and beyond. This exposure became the premise that allowed me to take my business to the next level and secure contracts on a scale that I had not imagined. Dennis E. Cook, CEO of WES Health Systems, and Kathleen Rogers, president of Earth Day Network, were instrumental in the growth of Galaxy. I am grateful for the life-changing opportunities that these individuals afforded me without a proven-track record. Their experience allowed them to become vested in the passion and commitment that was brought to every project that Galaxy proposed and delivered. I encourage all entrepreneurs to operate your business with honor and honor will be returned to your business in due season.

Relinquish Your Desires
MONICA HUGHLEY

"I've always been that kind of person who has been very driven, goal oriented, and really just tried to make a way and succeed in life. My goal was always to define my own success and make it happen. I think I have done pretty well in that respect," says Monica.

Reaching financial goals has always been somewhat important to Monica as well, but the older she gets the less important certain things become. "As a society, we put so much emphasis on material things and those things are the least important in life." The most difficult thing for her was to face being a single-parent and raising her daughter. She made certain sacrifices so her daughter could live a privileged life and experience the things that she was afforded and more. That was an important issue for her. She had always wanted to be married. "During that process of working, you hope to find that someone to share that with, you know? Marriage was very important part of my upbringing and something that I desired."

"I think as women, we sometimes lose ourselves in our career; we have to be this and that, and make a certain amount of money. At the end of the day you find that it's just money, it's stuff and it's not going to love you back, talk to you, help you when you're sick or be there for you when you need a shoulder to cry on—it's giving you nothing back."

When she had her own business, she says that she went through failed relationships with people. "Part of it was probably because of my strength as a woman. Truthfully, I didn't take too much crap from to many people. I think sometimes when a woman is in business, men are intrigued by it, but they're also intimidated by it. And, that can be a recipe for a failed relationship. Both people can't wear the pants and at some point, the man wants to be ahead of the situation."

"It has to be the right man. It can't be someone who will be manipulative. It has to be somebody with integrity, strength, and compassion." Those are all the attributes that were lacking in the people that she was choosing to become involved with.

"One day while I was at my bank, I had developed a business relationship with my banker, as you should if that's who you're doing business with. So we eventually became friends. He was a Christian man and we would talk about all kinds of things. One time he told me, you know Monica 'If you want different results you have to do different things and make different choices.' That resonated with me and for some reason the light bulb went off. From that point on, I said I was going to take his advice because I never had anybody say anything to me that was just so simple, yet so profound."

Immediately, she started to do all the things that she wanted to do; everything important to her that she had dreamed about. She wanted to travel abroad, so she went to Paris and London. "I decided to be me. If that meant going to dinner or a movie by myself, or travel, I would do just that. All these things had been holding me back before waiting for that special person, but not anymore."

The same went for the types of people that she chose to meet. "I decided to do something different. Every time I began to encounter a situation, I would ask myself *am I doing something different, or am I falling back into the same old thing?* Based on that question that I asked myself, I would adjust what it was that needed changing."

"It was when I decided to do something different that I met my husband. He was different. He wasn't uptight with a super A-type personality, nor Mr. Macho, I'm the center of the world guy. He wasn't Mr. Daddy Warbucks who believed everything revolved around him because he was doing well and thought he was the best thing since sliced bread."
He was a very kind, compassionate and loving person. "Even from a physical standpoint he was what I was attracted to, but his demeanor was different than what I was used to. Looking back, I know it sounds crazy, but as women we often say we want someone who looks a certain way… but he's too nice. We immediately put ourselves on alert thinking there's no possibility this can be true. Instead we should realize that we are worthy of all things that God has for us in a mate and what is this crazy notion that a man is too nice?

We went on our first date and one of the most important things happened; I talked and he listened to me. I found that so refreshing. I probably talked his ear off…LOL! It was the little things that he remembered during our chats that he later followed up that were so special. He was so alert to hearing what was important to me, hearing things that made me happy or even things that I was concerned with. I remember thinking oh, he's just too nice. Then I stopped myself and said what did your friend say, *you want different results, then do different things.*

This had come after years of praying for God to send me someone, asking him where was my husband, you know just crying over this one and crying over that one."

"I would say that has been one of the most defining moments in my life. When I decided to change my thoughts and actions, God brought a wonderful man into my life. Someone that was totally different than what I was looking for from a personality standpoint who complemented me perfectly.

He's a good guy, we've worked together as a family, and he's encouraged me in my career and my studies. I've encouraged him in his career and we sacrifice a lot. But it's been a true blessing because we are working together as a family unit. All those things I desired in a mate and in my life have come to pass. I have to thank God everyday for giving me exactly what I *needed*. Sometimes you just don't know what you need so you have to be open to receive the blessing. I say to women all the time to just open up ourselves to other possibilities. Sometimes the blessing doesn't come in the package we expect (or sometimes it does). You may be amazed to see what God can do."

MEET THIS WISE WOMAN OF COLOR:

Monica Hughley is a multifaceted woman. She is a dedicated wife and mother of three beautiful children, a child of God, a daughter, sister, and a friend. She is a rotarian and a dedicated philanthropist. Monica has a B.A. from Purdue University and a MBA from Indiana Wesleyan University. Her career path has taken her on the road of entrepreneurship in many different capacities. She was the director of the Women's Enterprise

Program, Indiana's First Women's Business Center at the Women's Bureau in Fort Wayne, Indiana.

Prior to that, Monica directed Syracuse University's South-side Entrepreneurial Connect Project and South Side Innovation Center, a business incubator in conjunction with the Whitman School of Management at Syracuse University. She is also a business owner, owning one of the only women-owned chemical distribution companies and was a certified MBE, WBE and SDBE. Her business was successfully awarded many government contracts with many municipalities, state, and federal agencies; and she has conducted business with countries in Asia and South America.

Monica now owns Hughley Consulting and does small business and program consulting. In her spare time she enjoys learning foreign languages, reading, and traveling the world to exotic locations with her husband.

She Had the Vision to Do It
TAMEIKA BURRELL

Sixteen years of marriage was a long time for this once teenager who became pregnant at 16 years old. It was almost two years after meeting him when she became a mom to a daughter and around four years later when she became a wife to her husband. To her it seemed like she was devoted to her family most of her life; that's all she knew.

It's no surprise that when Tameika got a divorce she had to find herself and God. She says, "I was able to finally see me as God saw me." She always knew who He was, but her relationship with Him had further to flourish.

After a year of separation, although hoping for reconciliation, her husband came to her and said, "I don't want to do this anymore." She asked him, "What is it about me?" She thought that she must have been awful; his actions were a reflection of something wrong with her, given their long history.

One evening while seemingly all alone, she sat there asking God, "What am I supposed to do without this man?" She said he had been her best friend since she was 16 and she had no idea how she was supposed to live without him.

It would be one night about a year after the divorce when she realized that God had been protecting her all along. She ended up finding out that secretly had another child about three years after their marriage. Upon learning of this, she realized that her marriage was doomed from the start. She admits that, "I prayed for that young man," She goes on to say, "Be careful for what you pray for because you get all that it comes with." While trying to deal with the hurt and pain of a failed marriage, God came to her and gave her a vision that she would be just fine and that she would testify about it in front of her church on Watch Night Service. She thought to herself *I know He must be joking.* She was not the type to share her business, let alone at her church with about 10,000 members. But, no matter how much she fought it, He kept placing that vision especially during her most difficult times.

Tameika did not share God's vision with anyone so when New Year's Eve came in and it was time to give a testimony, she marched herself right up to the microphone and was obedient in pouring it all out. She felt like it was an out of body experience and all she could ask God silently was, "Are you kidding me, you're that real?"

People came from all over her congregation to tell her how they were moved by her testimony. To her surprise some also shared that they were going through similar situations. She felt comforted hearing them confirm God's Word that *she would be okay.* She says the news spread quickly, because by the time she was home her phone was ringing off the hook with *people who heard.* All she could tell them was, "I just had to do it in front of God's people." Her experience with God has been remarkable.

She knows today that God is there for her and that He will watch over her life. She says the experience was profound and remains a prominent memory. She knows who she is and she has no worries about how her future may end up. She even says that, "If I'm single for the rest of my life, that's alright because my God has me."

MEET THIS WISE WOMAN OF COLOR:

Tameika D Burrell grew up in Prince George's County, Maryland, a predominantly Black middle class suburb in the Washington, D.C. area. She was raised by a single mother to whom she credits her independence, strength and not-so-quiet spirit (smile). At the age of 16, Tameika became a statistic: a teenage mother, although she would not allow her circumstances to define her nor would she succumb to the stereotypes that went along with it. In contrast, she graduated from high school as scheduled; graduated from Bowie State University four years later with love and support from her mother, family, and friends; and also married her child's father during that time.

It was not until her nearly-16-year marriage ended in 2009 that she realized that this journey called life is truly a blessed gift from GOD. After going through her divorce, probably one of the most difficult times in her life, she now rests in the full peace and love of God and continues to stand on His promises. Tameika is most proud and grateful for her 21 year old daughter, a senior at Hampton University, who is the reason why she lives and the absolute joy of her life. Now at 38 years old, Tameika meditates on Romans 8:28 as a banner for her life in which she continues to trust God and His will to be done on the rest of her journey.

She Was Finally Heard
LISA C. R.

Five and a half years ago, she separated from a marriage that was unhealthy. On record it's been officially two years since their divorce. Out of the marriage she was blessed to have two sons ages eleven and eight. "During the marriage I felt worthless and not worthy of anything. I left my relationship for my children and there wasn't much help and assistance when we were together," says Lisa.

"I questioned myself many times, asking if I should wait until my children reached a certain age. I knew though that if I wasn't in my right mind, how could I take care of them?" The best way for her to get through the scenario was to seek counseling. It was her husband that actually suggested seeking a marriage counselor and he selected one. He became unhappy with what was being said and decided that he no longer wanted to go. It was a situation where if the counselor didn't agree, he was unhappy; but if she did, he was okay. "I continued going alone and that helped me look at myself with a different set of eyes. I was also able to get a different perspective of what was going on; something other than what was in my mind. I was being abused," Lisa recounts. Verbally abused.

"It was through counseling that I mustered the courage to ask my husband to leave. I was finding out I was worth something and of some use. I started feeling like somebody needed me – my children. My thoughts were very confused at first. Here I was a professional guidance counselor working with children and couldn't see a way out for myself. Since I work in a therapy environment every day I knew someone had to deal with my kids, but who? I started believing, no weapons formed against me – it's done. I had to believe that just to be his wife was not my soul purpose.

I had to give to my children as well as those I worked with. The situation made me second-guess a lot of things. I started realizing my worth, my purpose in life and thinking more about how I help others (my children and family).

I knew that my purpose in life was to give back to our children in the world. I believed in being there for children regardless of their situations. I felt they have to have someone to talk to and I worked tirelessly to build a rapport with them. In my past I worked with a group of 15-30 year-old girls that I called my girls. I was and still am their go-to-person for things. They were able to embrace our conversations. Today, they are prosperous and successful in life."

At the school she is a guidance counselor for grades K-8, which includes children ages five to thirteen. "If the children are looking for something or someone, in addition to knowing God, I teach them to reflect on the things they've seen before that were positive and to look back within themselves to find the good." She nurtures them, because they need to hear from someone else other than themselves. She believes when outside eyes take notice it's sometimes easier to get through. Those that are closest sometimes may not see and hear the whole piece that the children try to communicate.

"I know even for myself when I sought counseling, it was a different viewpoint then what my family offered me," says Lisa. She would walk in the house and her sister would say, "You ain't fixed yet? Are you still going to talk to that counselor?"

"I chose to put my children in counseling as well and they have a healthy relationship with their father. I am glad that I broke free from that mindset. I grew up with two parents and my parents worked through it. They weren't perfect, but sacrificed for me. I know I made many excuses to stay in the beginning. There was always one more thing to do, like finish school first or do this or that first. I knew that things turned bad when we weren't talking and if we were he was argumentative and called me names. He had control over my belongings and was like I said violent, verbally abusive, controlling and powerful.

It took me three years to really decide this is it. I had to turn to spiritual and motivational readings and speeches. They helped me to feel good about myself. I especially felt myself move when I listened to Joel Olsteen, his words helped me to find my purpose and he reiterated the message to me – this then began to happen wherever I went," she shares.

MEET THIS WISE WOMAN OF COLOR:

Born and raised in Brooklyn, the youngest girl of three, I had aspired to be a lawyer in my younger years yet somehow I ended up an educator. After 19 years in the educational field, I now have to say it was my calling.

I began my educational career as a middle school teacher. The social emotional needs of my students were not being met. I wanted to do

She Was Finally Heard

something to change that. I wanted to make a difference. I always felt if I only touched one child's life, I was successful. I became a school counselor.

As a mother of two boys and many adopted children, I continue to help our children set realistic goals and attain them. I continue to be their advocate. They are our future and I am proud.

~ Lisa

20 She Turned Left to Get Right
SABINA MOISE

Ms. Sabina was 18 years old and it was the first time in her life that she was out of her house and on her own. She welcomed Florida with open arms and big dreams. She felt honored to be there as an undergraduate in college on scholarship. Her plans were to complete the pre-med program and one day become a doctor...she had the next 10 years all planned out.

Coming from Brooklyn, this young lady was the middle child of three. As a Haitian American she was raised tight, but it wasn't a problem for her; after all she always had good grades. Her family was supportive and they taught her to be responsible and do the right thing. She was well on her way with a head-strong personality.

In Florida, she stayed with relatives and commuted to school daily. She had to learn her own way around. She says she began to feel alone and wasn't learning how to get through college. It didn't help that she had a photographic memory so she didn't need to nor did she learn how to study while in high school. As college would have it the challenge became harder. And as it became more difficult she started seeking the wrong interests. She found the wrong crowd.

Sabina says she found herself a "Jamaican friend" as her mom would call her. Although her mom wasn't there the first year that they met, her mother eventually moved to Florida by her sophomore year. By then, the friendship had been solidified. Her mom tried to protect her numerous times from her friend, because she could see right through the situation enough to know it wasn't a healthy relationship to have. Sabina says her mom thought her friend was a leech.

When Sabina originally entered college she was heavily into sports and physical fitness, but her friend was into socializing more and hanging out with guys. Her mom was right. Influenced to party, she quickly learned the ropes and became more social. She was also known as the driver. Nothing good came of her behavior as she soon started defying her parents and failing classes.

It all turned wrong when she was introduced to a young man through her friend. It was the roommate to her friend's boyfriend. This would be Sabina's first official boyfriend. She's not really sure why, but she was intrigued by his attitude where, "He didn't take crap from anybody." After becoming serious she realized that he was not the right person for her. She says she then experienced cheating, disrespect, and embarrassment when he talked to other girls in front of her and more. She left him but her friend convinced her to stay with him. That's when her self-esteem took a downward spiral. She began questioning the fact that he befriended multiple women, but again, her friend pushed her to stay. Sabina never stood up for herself and went on to failing practically every class. She eventually lost her scholarship.

She remembers trying to regain control, but to no avail she had already lost so much. By then she had stopped playing sports and found it hard to go back to her family – she had no other outlet. As if it could get any worse,

Sabina met her ex-boyfriend's nephew. To her he was eye candy. They never had a conversation back when she was with her boyfriend but they began getting to know one another once the boyfriend became her ex. She said, "I needed to be needed. I needed something to do and someone to care for." This one was two years younger than her, but he was no saint. She ended up buying the liquor for them as they spent a lot of time drinking and wasting time. She says, "He was going nowhere fast." He smoked and got high; and she would get a contact high. She had felt majorly unworthy. He too didn't respect her and while she steadily took care of his needs, he raised his voice at her often. She said it was verbal abuse, but she had tooted it up to a high tolerance of pain.

It was eight months into the relationship and she rarely brought him home. "My mom would have seen right through it," Sabina says. So she stayed away from home all night as much as possible.

Things only got worse when Sabina was fired from her job. She was often late or didn't show up at all. She stayed with him on the couch watching television, wasting time. After all, he had no job and his mom supported him. She says she drank wine coolers all day and to make matters worse, she found out that she was pregnant.

Sabina started thinking, "How am I going to leave this situation? He accepted me all broken up." She still needed affection and felt too ashamed to get an abortion. So she stayed for a bit.

As the changes took place in her body she started standing up for herself. She says, "(She) was going to make changes...." The hormonal changes changed her and she realized she had "much more important things to worry about." She decided to keep her baby. Then, he accused her of cheating on him. When she was trying to make a change in her life, it came to an end when he asked her, "Are you sure it's mine?"

It had taken a while to get there, but "the light bulb went off to do the right thing." She knew he wasn't her future, so she told her parents she was pregnant. She left and never saw him again. Soon after, Sabina gave birth to a premature son.

Her baby was a blessing to her life. She was put under during delivery so she could have a C-Section. While she was under she remembers having a conversation with Jesus and was told *you are of good intentions.* "He told me it's ok, I accept you, and I know where your heart is," she clearly recounts. She says with each day that passed by she became more blessed. "Without God on my side, I wouldn't have believed it. He touched my life."

She found a great job and went back to school. She learned from the experience and that gave her strength. She also realized that she "didn't have to let go of a dream."

Even though her child had developmental delays, she says it didn't deter her. She kept pushing forward. She earned her undergraduate degree and in her early 30s returned to graduate school full-time. Sabina is still working on completing medical school. Today, Sabina is a personal trainer and lifestyle coach. She uses her past experiences to motivate others, helping them to make transformations in their lives.

MEET THIS WISE WOMAN OF COLOR:

I was born and raised in Brooklyn, New York, by Haitian parents, to be strong, independent, and faithful in the Church. I completed my undergraduate degree at Barry University. After having a child and marriage, I followed my dreams to become a medical doctor. Though the journey is challenging due to family and financial demands, I continue to strive to complete my medical degree along with my MBA in health care administration, in two years' time.

I am the owner of B Fit Consulting, LLC, a personal training and fitness consultation company. I work one-on-one with people who are new to fitness and I provide consultations for individuals experienced in training. All programs are customized to the individual and created to take the guesswork out of designing a fitness plan and nutritional advice. I use what I have learned through my own experiences to provide lifestyle coaching and support, for the future of a healthy nation.

~ Sabina Moise, CPT B Fit Consulting, LLC

21 She Realized She Deserved Better
MICHELE BELL

Her parents were divorced and she was raised by her mother. Her mother was going through many hard times financially and emotionally; she did not appreciate having to raise her and her sister without the help of her father on a day-to-day basis. Michele believed that her mom was unhappy, since she constantly drilled her dislike for parenting in their heads. From the age of 13, she remembers hearing "when you get 18, you are getting out of here."

The conversation never changed over the years, no matter what accomplishments were made in school, her mom's words never diverted from *when you get 18, you're out of here.* She had to believe her mom's sincerity, because she forced them to use their summer job money, buy their own groceries, and cook their own food, in addition to doing normal chores.

Michele (Shell for short) was skipped a grade in school, so she graduated from high school a year earlier at the age of 17. She graduated from high school on June 16, 1983; on June 17th, both she and her sister went and got jobs at the nearby Wendy's in downtown Philadelphia with the idea of being able to financially contribute to the household. "To our surprise, on July 1st our mother had rolled. She moved out of our apartment and had taken all of her furniture leaving us with only our bedroom furniture," Shell recalls.

At the time we were living in high-rise projects where children's names were not individually placed on the lease. The lease was between the Philadelphia Housing Authority and her mother. She says, "Fortunately, she left a note stating that our names were not on the lease and we would need to find someplace to live." At the age of 17, Shell was now trying to locate an apartment for them to live.

"I felt like, what did I do wrong as a child? Is this something that a mother would do? And, of all people, how can your mother leave you? I had already experienced the fact that my father was not there on a day-to-day basis, and I felt like I didn't have a father or a mother. I was feeling like an orphan in the world with no one to turn to. At my age, that was not a normal life," she shared. Her friends were dating and going to the movies and she was paying bills and trying to make sure that she and her sister worked enough hours each week to handle all of their expenses.

"I look back and now see the blessings that came out of this ordeal. Although I still feel blessed, I realize that my sister and I were also trying to deal with abandonment issues. I learned later that we were traumatized by it. We were both desperately trying to silently cope with this issue and its effects for nearly 20 years," reflects Shell.

It wasn't until she was grown that she realized that was abandonment. She thought that because they were able to stay afloat and survive, get better jobs, make more money, buy cars and live in beautiful apartments – she was fine. She was far from it. On the outside she had it together, on the inside she was falling apart. The experience had a major affect on the both of them, but the biggest effect was how they dealt with relationships.

She Realized She Deserved Better

They both had no problem meeting or being attracted to men. Her father's involvement in her life made selection for her, cautious and specific. She always managed to choose good men. They were never abusive emotionally, physically or mentally. However, they weren't good for her. Her sister's choices were totally opposite. While she sought those that would not be able to offer a lifetime with them, her sister held on (or tried to) so tightly that she became clingy with individuals that were not worth holding onto.

They had the same issue, but had two different ways of handling it. She believed that abandonment was extremely difficult to adjust to and being abandoned by a parent (in this case, her mother) made it harder to dismiss. Her choice of guys, were men with financial wealth, but were generally involved with other women. While she didn't always know this from the beginning, because of them lying, when she found out it didn't rattle her to leave them alone. She says, "If they weren't married they were probably living with someone or in a long-term relationship with someone else." She believed these relationships felt safe for her.

By choosing men that were involved with another women, she knew that they were not going to concern themselves with anything long-term and she could cut them off when she was tired, without feeling bad; or she would not expect them to stick around for a long period of time. With single men, she would usually end the relationship right after they had their first disagreement. She would decide on her own that she would leave a man alone to avoid someone else leaving her first. "Without me realizing it I was demonstrating a huge fear, which I faced again and again, abandonment," says Shell.

Her religious background at the time was scattered, because her mother's household was Jehovah Witness and her father's was Seventh Day Adventist. For the most part, by the time she was on her own, she thinks she rebelled against any religion not sure what religion was right. Shell declares undoubtedly, "But God has a way of placing the right people in your life at the right time."

"When the time was right, a coworker and I were collaborating on beginning a drill team in the West Philadelphia area. She wanted to have it in the basement of her church, where she attended. I thought the idea was excellent and went with her to discuss the matter with her pastor. Little did I realize this meeting would put me front and center of where I needed to be – in church. I went from coming to church strictly for the drill team practices to attending a week long revival service, and from there I was baptized and became a member."

"When I became involved and worked with the drill team and other ministries in the church I started learning that I also needed to work on me and my relationship with God. I would always pray and believe that my prayers were heard over the years. I knew that some of the situations that I had placed myself in, while growing up, that God was surely on my side and offered his hand of protection on my life. The more I learned about his goodness and love for me despite my imperfections, the more I wanted to be a better person for Him. I was thankful for all that He had done for me and needed to prove it to Him. Certain things had to change in my life. My relationships with men that were seeing other people or were married had to stop. I didn't want to be someone that God would not find favor with. I didn't want to block my blessings any longer."

She Realized She Deserved Better

Shell says that it took some time, but she's so thankful to God for giving her the strength to take charge of her life. She didn't have to allow someone else and her fears of abandonment to continue to empower her life. She had to forgive her mother. And while she didn't receive an explanation about why she left, she did realize that she was not born perfect. She also understood at that point that everyone was not meant to be a parent. She realized that everyone had to answer to God on his or her own merits. Her concern was her personal relationship with Him.

She continued to live her life trying to do the right thing. When her son came along and she was raising him by herself, she tried to imagine what her life would be like if she just walked away from him when he turned 16. She is thankful that she never could. It was something that she could never imagine doing, no matter how hard it was at the time. She knew in no way, shape or form that he would be ready to take on the world. "My job as a parent was to be able to prepare him to be a responsible adult. I could not prepare him if I wasn't in his life. No matter how long it took for him to be ready, I was going to be there for him," Shell said.

Her blessings continued as she continued to do the right thing. She received a man of her own. She believed that he was going to be her husband after their first date. She had never experienced the connection that she had with him, with anyone in her past. She actually felt butterflies in her stomach when meeting up with him for a date. She always enjoyed the times that they spent together learning about one another. But despite the thrill and satisfaction and belief that he was the one, she still had the issue of abandonment that would rear its ugly head.

Shell's relationship progressed toward marriage. She had normal ups and downs in the relationship that often led her to the threat of leaving. She was faced time and time again to deal with her fears of abandonment. She realized later on that she was trying to sabotage a relationship when she really didn't have to. Her fiancé was concerned not knowing if she would stay with him. It was at that time that she had to check herself and look in the mirror. She says it was always easier to place the blame on someone else. "It's harder to look in the mirror and face reality. See what everyone sees in you."

She felt this *time she was not going to lose the one God gave her because she was stuck on stupid.* She told herself, "Shell you have got to get yourself together, this is not the one that you want to lose." She knew in her heart that he was the one for her and she learned that he was someone she deserved. "Not only did I deserve a man that could give me his love but I also deserve to be with someone who was not afraid to do so for the rest of their lives."

Now that she was in church she learned that her responsibilities included living a life that would be pleasing to God and she also learned about having faith. Her faith was strong and she trusted there was nothing that God wouldn't do. "He assured me that if I had faith He would be able to help me to continue to overcome the issue of abandonment by strengthening me. He continued to reveal to me how much love I had to give to another person and how I was capable of accepting an individual loving me. I believe that my faith and relationship with God are equally as strong. My faith allowed me to be readied by God to be a wife and only want someone who was husband material."

Shell is happy to say that not only did he become husband, she has been blessed that their marriage is filled with love and respect for one another.

MEET THIS WISE WOMAN OF COLOR:

Michele is a wife and mother of two boys, residing in Philadelphia PA. She has a 23-year-old son who is currently living on his own and a 14-year-old stepson. She recently left the insurance industry, after twenty plus years, to pursue her passion for helping people in the human services field. She has also recently returned to school and is studying Communications and Social Sciences at the University of Pennsylvania. As a student she had the opportunity to join their student run radio station WQHS.org and she has been living her dream as a radio personality sharing urban and R&B music along with offering advice on love and relationships. She believes in love and thinks that women need to be empowered in order to make better decisions on partners and those individuals they choose to share in their lives.

Michele believes in and shares with others her love for men. Her mission is not about male bashing. She knows that there are still a number of good men in the world. Hence her business name, *Sounds Like Happy*. She is adamant that women are the ones that make the choices and that men would be more willing to "act right" if women would have expectations for them to reach. When you expect nothing, you get nothing. Men will only do what you allow them to do. Therefore it is up to us, as women to get them to do more and expect more. Why settle for less when you can get more? She desires and is moving towards making this clear to every woman that she comes into contact with that is still not aware of her worth. As a queen, she believes that everyone deserves to find her king. She believes that it starts with learning about self. Once you know who you are and what you want and don't want, it is easier to determine what kind of person you want.

22 Bring About What You Think About
KRISTELL DOUGLAS

There was a period in Kristell's life when she felt like she was not in control. She was hanging out partying a lot. This was back in the 80's when the music was so good. It was the thing to do back then. Party, drink, smoke and date, date, date. She was dating different guys and never stayed with one for too long. No commitments. She was with her friends having a ball and she never really realized how fast she was moving. One night they went to Studio 54 in New York City and partied hard, drinking all night. She decided to get high and had some cocaine. She felt euphoric and danced all night. After the club, they went to Cozy Soup and Burger in the wee hours because they were so hungry. When she got back to her Brooklyn apartment, she couldn't sleep. Her heart was racing and she was very uncomfortable. She started to feel like she couldn't breathe and couldn't calm her heart down. So she lay down and closed her eyes and asked God to let the fast, heart beating stop so that she could go to sleep. She promised that if He did that for her she would never get high again. For her that was it. Fearing she would turn out like her drug addict mother, she sought out a therapist through the employee assistance program at her good job. She also told her sisters since she could tell them anything – she had to gain control – and she did.

About two years later she met her soon-to-be husband. They had plans to marry the next year, but she found out that she was pregnant before the wedding. Her daughter was born and they got married a few months later in April 1992. Later that year, she then had to put her mother in rehab. Her mother was really strung out on drugs, doing crack and heroin. She didn't come around, she was gone and it seemed like she just didn't care about her granddaughter or Kristell.

One day Kristell called her mom and she didn't sound right. After she hung up, she had a feeling that she had to go and find her mother. She asked her neighbor to watch her daughter, then got into her car and drove around the neighborhood where she heard that her mother was living to see if she could just see her somewhere. She was so tired of looking that she decided to park and sit on the block for a while. Then, she saw somebody walking down the block, but the person was so far away that she couldn't tell who it was. The person had a big coat with a hood and it was almost 80 degrees outside. She was thinking, "Who is this with this big coat on out here in this heat?" By then, she knew it was a woman. The lady was just walking and looking up in the sky. But, as the person got closer and closer, she realized it was her mother. She was dirty, she was skinny, and she had a black eye. As she walked closer to the car she was looking at her daughter but didn't know it was her. So, when she reached the car, Kristell got out of the car and walked over to her. She stopped, saw Kristell, and held her head low. She was really ashamed. Kristell said, "Hi ma" and she answered her, "Hi baby." Kristell said, "Ma where you going, where have you been? "She said I've been around. " Kristell asked her was she okay, and she said, "Yeah" as she always did, never wanting her girls to worry about her. She then tried to walk back the other way to where she came from. Kristell said, "No, get in the car and let's go for a ride." She got in the car and they went for a ride. They talked for a while. Kristell asked her, "Do you want to die?" Because if so, then she wanted her mother to let her know so they could all be prepared. She told her that she was tired of worrying about her. She said to her, "We love you and just don't know what to do, so if you are ready let me take you someplace and get you some help." Kristell continued telling her mom, "This is it… you have a granddaughter now and if you don't get yourself together and get straight, I will never let you see her. I will not let you be around her this way."

Her mom had so many demons; being given away by her real parents to her aunt and uncle to raise her and still being around her real siblings, being raped at the age of nine, not knowing who her real father was, and never feeling good enough. Kristell told her that she couldn't imagine what she must have had festering inside of her but that it was time to put it in the Lord's hands. She told her, "You have four daughters that love you and you have a granddaughter now." So the question was would she go? And she did. Kristell found out later on that her mom was raped in an alley the night before she found her and that's how she had gotten beat up. That was the hardest thing she ever had to hear – just listening to her mother during her intake at the rehab program recounting what happened to her and all the different drugs she had consumed. "Mmmm," with her eyes closed, Kristell moans while shaking her head.

Her mother's journey helped shape her life, making Kristell a stronger woman and better mother to her daughter. It made her open to learn from any situation and to use those learnings to teach her daughter how to be a just as strong of a woman. Determined to teach her daughter that she could do anything she put her mind to, she has instilled in her confidence, encourages her to be unique, but most of all to love God and herself. She's never wanted her daughter to think that she isn't able, but that she is capable. She tells her constantly, "You are beautiful" and "You bring about what you think about."

Today Kristell's mom is very different. She is one of the mightiest women she knows. She's suffered from kidney failure, was in a coma for a short time and came out of it. After a brief waiting period her mom got a kidney transplant. Kristell says, "She is so blessed to have gotten one so soon. People often wait years for a match. She turned her life around and it's now been six years. She has a partner and is in a place mentally where she wants to live. She's afraid to die. She's doing everything she can to extend her life." She told her mom, "You are blessed and highly favored and God has you here for a reason. He kept you for a purpose." Each day, Kristell's mom reads the Daily Word, calls her and her sisters to tell how proud of them she is, and shares how much she loves them.

MEET THIS WISE WOMAN OF COLOR:

My name is Kristell Sigmone Douglas. I am a fabulous 50-year-old baby boomer. Born and raised in Queens, New York, I currently reside in Atlanta, Georgia where I have lived for the last 11 yrs. I have always dreamed of being an entrepreneur since I was a teenager – I was one of those kids that had a lemonade stand, my own summer school in my basement, a dance class in my backyard and encouraged all the kids on my block to join in. I have always been "The Gatherer."

I am still working at building my own business while working in the corporate world and it's happening slowly, but surely. Some folks that know me call me a professional network marketer. So yes, I have been involved with a few (LOL, maybe more) network marketing companies and it's only because I know that they DO WORK. I have made a nice additional stream of income doing this. However, my passion is Teen Mentoring. I worked with a non-profit teen-to-teen mentoring organization called Girl Talk. It is based in Atlanta but has chapters all over the U.S. The founder and executive director, Haley Kirkpatrick, started it in 2002 and its mission is to help young teenage girls build self-esteem, develop leadership skills, and recognize the value of community service and giving back.

I started a chapter as a parent advisor in Lawrenceville, Georgia because I wanted my then high school aged daughter, Samantha, to be involved in something positive and then her friends joined as well. We did some pretty amazing activities and community service projects. I am so proud of all the girls who are all now doing well in college. I stay in touch with Girl Talk and hope to start another chapter soon or to start my own. It goes a long way. We didn't have that growing up but we did have Aunties dancing school (now known as Movement of the Children Dancenter- Queens, New York). That was fun! I love life and feel so blessed. I am passionate and I love helping people. God has blessed me with a wonderful husband, a beautiful daughter, a loving family and friends. I am on my way and claiming success.

23 Be Good to Yourself
KAREN MOHAMMED

She was young and only 12 years old when she first realized that she had low self-esteem. Mighty early you may think to develop such a mindset, but this intuitive young lady knew what she knew. She felt as though she was different than the other girls; she didn't have the curvy body, she couldn't sing, and even dancing took her a long time to grasp. Her world was spinning.

She found herself trying to escape reality, so she began smoking marijuana. Her introverted personality didn't help either. On the outside she was a fly girl dressed as stylish as could be. She would hide her feelings for years. At 17, her drug of choice escalated to hallucinogens. By then, she still didn't talk about her issues, but she knew how to party and have fun times with friends. By 24, she was hooked on crack cocaine. All her friends had turned away and she felt as though nobody was there for her… she thought she was supposed to just die.

Where could Karen turn? Her grandmother had mental illness and her mother was an only child. She had no aunts, uncles, cousins, nor a grandmother to talk to. Because of the conditions that her mom was raised in, she was unable to emotionally connect to her – her mom was rigid. And her dad, well he was in prison since she was three. Amazingly so, her mom was serious about her getting to school and doing well. She pushed her to get up on time, attend classes, and checked her homework. Her mom was the reason why she received her high school diploma and graduated on time.

For years she craved affection. All she ever wanted was for her mom to be there for her. She was certainly no daddy's girl and she was a different sheep out of her other siblings who did very well.

There she was growing up in East New York, Brooklyn, 18 years old, pregnant, and on drugs. She didn't know she could stop. "It was never a thought. I went to sleep and woke up to the drugs. Every day I was high," says Karen. It would take an act of God for her to get her life in order.

She ended up having two more children all by the same father. Her youngest son was a newborn at the time when they were all forcefully taken away from her. A judge gave a court order to have her children removed and put into the court system. She had to enter an 18-month drug rehab program to get them back. "I was angry as hell. I didn't want to stop. It was like a nightmare and the treatment was rigorous back then. It felt like prison…" Karen remembers.

"The treatment was cold, rigid and it broke you down then built you back up. It worked." Therapeutically she was healed and finally knew who she was. She says before that she was lost. Going there helped her to learn, to escape the drugs and feel. She met many good people and became more spiritual. Her whole life changed and she did a 360 turnaround.

With help from her children's father/her husband she was able to go back to school and pursue a college degree. She graduated from Columbia

University at the top of her class. She went on to get several certificates and a master's degree. She says, "There is no way, know how, 20 years ago I would have thought it was possible. I really wanted something for myself. I became motivated. You gotta want it, and you have to be good to yourself" Karen states. She wanted a better life for herself and for her children; an education and spirituality was the way for her.

Faith would have it that the same place that she started working at in an entry level position is the same place where she would become director many years later. All of her working life has been in the substance abuse field. She loves what she does and she enjoys helping other people. She's most passionate about working with women in the prison system. "My life was spared, and it could have been me. How can I judge?" she says.

Karen says she was handed a lifeline that released her to have phenomenal joy – her calling. "It's a yearning deep down like a fire and only God can give you that fire."

MEET THIS WISE WOMAN OF COLOR:

Karen Mohammed-Perry is an African American female who holds a position as a clinical director of a substance abuse treatment program. Karen has been in the substance abuse field for 18 years. She holds a master's degree in social work and a post master degree in advanced studies in treatment of alcohol and drug abusing clients. Karen is also passionate about serving the women in the NYC correctional facilities helping women to rehabilitate and change their lives around. Karen is committed to the women of color and has dedicated her life to serving others.

24 She Refused to Lay Down
LORRAINE LYNCH (LADY LOE)

Her skills on the basketball court landed her admission to Buffalo State College where she did very well. Unfortunately, there were no scholarships available because it was a Division III school. No one would ever know that this superstar had loans mounting as she played her behind off breaking several records. As she gained stardom on the campus grounds this star player started lavishing as the teachers' pet and found herself enjoying another kind of high – marijuana.

Inevitably, she had no other choice but to transfer schools due to the financial hardship. She would find herself at the New York Institute of Technology where she quickly regained stardom and picked up old habits. Only this time she began to dibble in sniffing cocaine. Lady LOE knew that she started spiraling out of control when her tolerance level escalated.

Life went on for the college freshman. She was gay and lived her life openly although her parents didn't approve. With the desire to feel loved by her family she thought that she would give a guy a chance at least once. She met him in school and he sold her on the word *love*. Soon after, he asked her to have a baby and she willingly did so. She says it was absolutely no mistake that she became pregnant. She was hoping to find what she was missing in her life. While pregnant she was red-shirted, allowing her to remain on the team without having to play until the following year. She stopped smoking and doing drugs all for her baby. It wasn't long before her relationship went sour. She had no other choice but to turn to her parents. To her surprise her parents were more than willing to help her raise the baby so that she could go back to school.

Home life wasn't easy being a young mother witnessing dysfunction and addiction. Both of her parents were alcoholics and her brother was also smoking. She says once she was home, her habit switched to crack, but somehow she managed to hold on to a job. She recalls one day seeing her brother smoking near the back door. She asked him if she could *hit that*. After she inhaled a few times, she felt like demons were around her and she could see them. Later in her life she wrote a song about it called *Dark Side*. Many things were going through her head during those times. Most importantly she had a feeling of low self-esteem, she was gay, no one understood her, she wasn't feeling accepted, and her parents were alcoholics.

Her son was now a few months old, both of her parents were drunks, and she was feeling lower by the day. She cannot recall a reason, if there even was one for a time when her dad told her, "Get out!" She does know that she was unable to process what he was saying. With her pride high it was too much for her to stay. She took her son, packed up his belongings, left and got a train. She found herself sitting in Washington Square Park alone on a bench with her son asleep on her chest. She says she sat there rocking him the entire night. A passerby asked her if she needed money because he had seen her there every time he walked by. She said the stranger gave her between $20-$40 for something to eat. She took the money and went to a nearby diner where she asked the waitress to heat up her baby's milk. Her girlfriend ended up calling her that morning and she told her all that had happened through the night. Lady LOE said that she didn't call her the night before, because she really didn't want to go to her house to stay since her girlfriend's three brothers smoked crack. She knew that even though she smoked, too, she couldn't put her baby in a higher risk than he already was.

With no place else to go she ended up there anyway. She stayed with them in a three-bedroom apartment in Uptown Harlem. In total there were six people in the house. Shortly thereafter, she was fortunate to find a good job and was able to pay to stay. She often helped her girlfriend's mother with rent, because the brothers smoked up all the money. She said, "I can't be evicted again." It was a stressful time for her, the majority of her money was going to the household she had become part of; she was also smoking.

On a quest, she went to a cop where there was a sting and she was arrested. She says that was one of the biggest turning points of her life. There she was sitting in jail on a Friday where she would spend at least the whole weekend. It was dirty; women were lying on the concrete floor. "All kinds of women were in there and the smell was horrible." She recounts in her mind her only thought was, "I ain't lying on this floor." That's what she said, but she had no other choice but to join them. Exhausted from standing she "couldn't wait for a spot to clear." She waited anxiously for the guards to take someone out so she could jump in the empty spot. She put her coat down and took the spot; the weekend felt like a lifetime. She had never been arrested in her life and she was feeling shame and guilt. She says she *can still hear the sound of the big steel doors close.* She remembers vividly watching women get bullied and shaken down. Her worst account was trying not to watch women use the toilet in the holding cell. It was horrific. By the time she went before the judge, she was bound and in pain, because she refused to *go* the entire weekend. She says, "It was (also) an embarrassing feeling to be in court with everyone looking at you."

After her court appearance she was moved to a double cell with a roommate where she'll never forget seeing her roommate have a seizure. She says it was just them in the tight space and the woman began shaking, foaming, and throwing herself about. She had no idea at that time what was going on. She just knew she was scared and started screaming for help. Once they took the roommate out, it was that moment that she asked herself, "Oh my God, what am I doing here?" She said, "I knew that was God, because I stopped everything and until this day, I've never gone back or touched another drug."

Never wanting to return, she was released and was able to go back home where her parents never remembered kicking her out. She went back to work and after some time she was able to save enough money to find a basement apartment *that was home*. She was determined not to ever live with anybody again. By now her baby was five-years-old. She says she was lucky to have such a well-managed son.

An opportunity to get away became one of the best days of her life. She went to visit a friend in Washington, D.C. who played basketball for the University of the District of Columbia (UDC). Looking for recreation while she was there her friend took her to her college court. She excitingly remembers, "I was balling really hard." The basketball coach came to the court to see what all the commotion was about. When the opportunity arose, the coach called her to 'come here'. She had no clue that the coach was there and in her New York mind she immediately thought, "Oh God, what did I do?" Her New York mentality was awfully cautious. The coach offered her a full-scholarship to attend the school and play. She had three years of eligibility so she took it. She called home from the coach's office to tell her dad and she laughs remembering what he said, "Get it in writing." And she did. She had a newfound determination and she knew it when she received two A's while she attended summer school to retake courses that were not transferable from her old college.

School started that December and Lady LOE received the best accommodations for her and her son. She couldn't wait to bring him there after she settled in. Lady LOE says at the age of 27, she was the oldest freshman on campus and in a dorm. But it turned out for the better as she was able to be a mentor to her roommates, teaching them respect.

Back home, her son was beginning to have problems in school. He was fighting and bringing toys to school to be liked. She knew it was time to move him to D.C. So she transferred him to a neighborhood school that was mostly an all-white school. He was eight-years-old. She recalls his first day of school when she knew it was a good fit. Her son came home excited and full of happiness talking up a storm about his day. She finally felt like she had done something right. The second day of school, the morning started off as usual. While in class she received a call from his school's principle. It was a call that would change her life, again. The principle told her that her son was trying to kill himself. He had held a pair of sharp scissors to his heart and threatened to harm himself. She rushed to the school to get her baby. She asked him, "What's wrong?" He asked her if she was going to beat him. She said she found that odd because she never hit him a day in his life. She told him, "No, I'm taking you for help. What's going on?" He told her, "The voices were telling (him) to do it." She had no idea what he was talking about. From there, he went to the children's hospital in D.C. for bi-polar treatment and care. She says it was rough, but she saw her child every day and most importantly she stayed involved in making decisions for him. Because of her past addictions and strong adversity to drugs, she researched everything she could about medications for her son and managed his intake.

That began her journey to social work. Her son eventually came home and was doing well. "It was not easy managing the transition and he often was a latchkey child," Lady LOE recalls. With the help of an unknown neighbor, a black elderly woman, he was able to be looked after while catching the bus and fed after school until she was able to return home from practice. She says, "Back then it felt safe to have people help you out. I didn't worry about the things you worry about now with strangers. The woman and her husband were a blessing."

By the time her son was in high school he was weaned off the medications, she never had any other problems. He graduated and went to Aim High. He's now 25-years-old serving in the Army in Afghanistan. This mom and advocate for children with mental illness has worked in the industry ever since her incident. She spends many days helping families to become educated on mental illness. She said, "It impacted my whole life, why wouldn't I do this?"

MEET THIS WISE WOMAN OF COLOR:
Lady LOE has now made her home in Washington, D.C. and has built

an enormous fan base within a short period of time. Lady LOE soon found herself making waves in the hip-hop music scene by performing continuously in the local D.C., Maryland, Virginia (DMV) region. Lady LOE has had the pleasure of opening for the well-known female R&B singer/songwriter Monifah, Project Pat of Three-6 Mafia, Babs of Bad Boy Records, De'Angelo Redman of Making Da Band 4, Scarface, and one of rap's legends, Slick Rick.

Lady LOE continues to pay dues in her community by being solely responsible for the creation of the theme song "60 Minutes of Hell" and "Ball Till U Fall" for D.C.'s own DC Divas all women, all tackle football team.

For music lovers, Lady LOE's third album will be released under her independent label, Love of Earth Entertainment. Meanwhile, you can listen to her past two collections "On Da Down LOE" and "RAW" available on iTunes. Lady LOE's ambition is to represent the past, present, and the future of the female hip-hop culture.

25 Blessed That They Call On Her
VERETTA DUDLEY

"I'm a 51-year-old New Jersian. I'm a sensitive social beautiful butterfly, and I can roll with those at the bottom of the barrel as well as those sitting in chairs fit for royalty. Getting along with people has never been a problem for me, it's the ways of the people that tend to disturb and dishearten me," says Veretta.

"I, like many women, have had that relationship with a man not fitting for me. Being in that relationship allowed me to lose myself for a moment. It was my daughter's father and the relationship lasted for some 20 years. It was September 11, 2005. One Sunday afternoon I just had had enough! I had been very depressed and I was going through some things. I decided this one day would go my way. Enough was enough. You know how they say when you are sick and tired of being sick and tired?

I said to him that he had to leave. I told him that he could do this the easy way on his own, be escorted by the men in blue, or my brother and brother-in-law could help him. Either way, it was a wrap and he needed to be gone by the time I got back. I left and went out to dinner with a friend of mine.

I was never married to him, but I didn't want my daughter to be one of the kids dealing with a broken family. I allowed him to take me to a dark place and I just couldn't do it anymore. I've been good sense then. *Now I'm Back.*"

She realizes that her purpose in life is to connect to people and help people. Veretta says, "This much I know." She has too many people that she knows who are in so many situations that need help every day. If you didn't know any better you may think that she was a certified psychologist. She helps a lot of friends that she's known for years. "I don't even have a job and I'm busy running around doing things for people and helping them like I'm working a 9 to 5 pro- bono. Then again maybe I am, if what I do or say changes something for someone, it's well worth it and that's my reward. Sometimes I find that helping others is a thankless job; especially if their family members have guilt and insecurities, it's a difficult balance. It's not so much that I want to do some of these things; I just do them well. So I do it just because."

"When I say I connect to people, I do. People are just drawn to me, of all races, ethnic backgrounds and so on." When she attended Essex County College in the evening, she had just completed a semester and probably was the oldest person in most of her classes. There were several young girls in the classes that she had no patience for, because they were extremely disrespectful. Yet, she connected with a few students. The situations that they were in were – unbelievable; problems in their household, and no one to listen to what they were going through. "It just baffles me when parents don't hear their child's cry for help. They were with me for just a semester and clinging to me. I was able to help. I would go to the guidance office, the financial aid office, and went on job interviews with kids. I helped them with homework and I didn't know these kids from Adam, but they called me on a regular. They called me Ma' Dudley. I cooked, invited them over to the house to talk…these were young girls and they were screaming for help softly."

The same thing happened to Veretta when she lived in Georgia back in 2007-2008. She knew she wanted to work with the youth. She mentored to young girls that attended school with her as well as those young ladies who didn't. She saw so many young girls that chose an alternative lifestyle and just didn't understand. "They hadn't even begun to live the life that was given to them. Some had two or three babies under the age of five, riding the bus, and talking on cell phones without a care in the world. Did I mention most of these young ladies were under 20 years of age? I met so many of the girls, talking, counseling and mentoring to them trying to give them some guidance that I sometimes felt like I was some social worker or something. The kids got to the place where they were like, Ms. V will help me; they just knew."

She did that a lot in Georgia. "I enjoyed it, because I knew I was making a difference in a young life." She has even received letters of recommendations from the staff down there because of what she was doing. "What a good feeling; somewhere along the line I knew this is what I'm supposed to be doing all the time. This is my calling."

She says, "For now, I need to complete something I've started. I have no degrees yet and I need a job so I'm looking. I'm still in school and completing a course in stenography – something I attempted back in 2006 and am now following through.

But like I said, my desire is to work with people and help them. I know I can start right now with just the girls in my family. We have about three or four younger ones who are good girls, going to college, doing right, nothing negative, but they can still use some guidance and so can I. I see so many of their friends who've gone the other way; it's tough to see them."

"Even with my own friends, we've grown up together and we all did our own things – some of us more than others. There are five that I remain friends with since the first grade. They've really gone through some things, but every one of them calls me and me them. One of them asked for my help with tutoring, I felt honored because she probably stopped going to school at an early age. I say these things to say, I know I'm here to help people and there are so many in need. In these instances, I just happen to be the person they call on. I guess they think Veretta may know a lil' something but the truth is I am sometimes all broken as well. I know for sure He brought me to it and He will bring me through it…God that is."

Going back to family, "I want to say we all have them and we already know we can't pick 'em. I love my family, I really do. But, we're just in different places. I know I'm different; a different person than I was probably 10 years ago when they saw me prior to separating from my daughter's father. I'm probably back to, if not, better than the person I was prior to that. In the same token, I'm different because I've matured and learned so much. I handle things differently now. *Spirit no longer broken…Amen.*"

"I have probably blown a couple of really good things based on how I reacted. I didn't think things through. I made decisions and just reacted on emotions. Doing that you get jacked up real quick. That put me in a couple of positions and places where I didn't want to be. Real talk, I could be working right now had I not made some hasty decisions in the past. But sometimes things come to you when they're due not because we want them. I like to believe that when I say no to something it's not the right time. I may not see the reason at the exact time, but later on down the road I see why. I could say *gosh I wasted time and could have been doing this or that* but not really. Sometimes I'm so busy that my mother has said to me, 'Well if you're not working where do you go everyday?' It's because I'm up, dressed, and out. *Time waits for no one.* I've found that I'm helping myself by helping others. It's what I'm supposed to be doing at this time."

"I try not to make apologies for my life. Nobody can carry guilt better than the person that's feeling it. Living is tough. Living day by day is tough. There was a time when I used to catch the bus at 7:30 in the morning; I would see some girls walking the street. I would come back at 8:30 p.m. and they were still out there walking. I would think *and I think I had a rough day.* So as much as I may have disliked the job I was doing, I wouldn't have traded places with them for nothing.

It's not easy, but you know what? I am glad to be here. I love my daughter and I am so blessed to have her. I know it's going to be okay. So many good things happen to me all the time and even though I fall short, I'm still making mistakes – but God is right here in my face.

I can't complain. I'm taking it day by day for what it's worth. Tomorrow isn't promised to anyone. Like I said, I'm glad to be here doing what I do and can do. I really am," Veretta assures.

MEET THIS WISE WOMAN OF COLOR:

First, I am a woman, God loving, spiritually connected, sensitive, and caring with a sharp tongue – kind though, and always lending a hand where I can.

Blessed That They Call On Her

Second, I am a mother who has not always been at her best, but getting better at it every day. And, I will protect my daughter with my life...I love her.

Third, I am a daughter, the oldest sibling, and a good friend indeed; very few of us get to have one. I am a continuous work in progress and embracing every moment.

26 She's Branching Out
JANET AUSTIN

"I haven't fully acquired my dreams just yet. While I'm in limbo, it's funny to me that everybody else sees me one way, but I don't see myself that way. I wonder what I portray to them. I don't feel like I wear a mask and I don't hold back, so what is it?" questions Janet.

A very successful business woman without a doubt, Janet has earned a bachelor's, two master's degrees, and held prestigious positions that she's proud of. She equates that to obtaining the goals that she set for herself and having a helping hand from God. Professionally, she has her life intact.

She will tell you that personally she puts herself behind to do for others. "I can always see what others need, but I need that push – I procrastinate and I know it's a sin." She talks to God on regularly asking for guidance. She ponders for answers asking, "Why do I work so hard for others and not for myself? How does this help Me? What is my purpose, God?"

She's had several dreams in her life from wanting to own a daycare to writing a children's book. She loves children and one day wants to motivate and teach them. This previously single mom raised her daughter and lived an independent life. She had to be responsible and make choices in the best interest of her child. There was no time to be a risk-taker; she needed stability and security. Today, her daughter is in her last year of college preparing to graduate. This proud mom knows that her daughter will be taken care of, which will allow Janet to follow her personal dreams.

She is not afraid to admit that "fear has been a big part" of her resistance to following her dreams. However, she knowingly says, "God is not about providing the spirit of fear, He's about offering love and a sound mind."

With God by her side she looks forward to journeying into volunteering with children and starting a family ministry, both having been on her heart for a long time. She's watched others struggle with not following the desires of their hearts and she feels that, too, has held her back; "I have fled long enough."

"I am transforming my thinking and learning from the past. There's nothing blocking me and I'm not stopping until I get there. I am seeking God for direction along the way. I know I have to get off excuses and find my way around it. I'm going to get it-watch!" Janet declares.

MEET THIS WISE WOMAN OF COLOR:

Janet Austin is a child of the most high God. Born and raised in the South Bronx, NY and 1 of 4 children. (The youngest and only girl). She attended and graduated from Syracuse University (SU) with a Bachelor's degree and thereafter worked as a nurse in several hospitals in the Bronx before going on to further her education. She then received 2 additional degrees from Iona College; A Master's of Science degree in Health Services Administration and an MBA. This young lady is a great believer in education. She strongly believes a mind is meant to be educated because there is so much in life to learn. She currently resides in the suburbs of New York with her husband and daughter (who currently attends her alma mater, SU).

Presently, Janet is working as a case manager in a well-known health insurance company in Manhattan, where she indirectly provides the utmost quality of care for the members. Janet works in the health field because she has a caring spirit and would like everyone to live their lives like it's golden in the best of health.

This woman continues to strive to succeed in her career and excel in life. Currently, she is working on several projects that will empower and develop others. She believes in putting God first in life and everything will fall into place as His plans are already in order for our lives. She continually seeks wisdom through her relationship with Christ, because this will pave the way for all of life's victories.

Matthews 6:33
Proverbs 3:5-6

~ Janet

27 A New Phase In Life
VERONICA ROLDAN-BURRIS

With a full-time job in Washington, D.C. and a family, she found balancing time to develop herself nearly impossible. But after 25 years of a rewarding professional career, Veronica's job was outsourced, and she felt it was time for a change. Leaving her comfort zone behind, she's no longer in Corporate America, instead she's enjoying the fruits of her labor in the tropical island of Puerto Rico. When I asked her if she went there to work, she said, "No, I'm taking the time to develop my spirituality and what a better place to find it."

At 57-years *young*, previously married, and now with grown children, it was time to concentrate on her. She says, "Enlightenment is hard to find." At this point of her life, she's enjoying the time that she has dedicated to educational development by reading spiritually uplifting and inspirational books, and gaining a better understanding of the people around her. She feels things are now clearer, and she knows this was the right path for her; living a life surrounded by nature, tranquility and spirituality.

At first, Veronica felt a bit lonely and lost in her walk; since her children had become of age where they no longer had the dependence they had as kids. She was no longer in a relationship and started living a life exploring her faith through several religious avenues. She says, "(She) has faith in God" – and as an adult she always felt that she wanted to expand her knowledge of other beliefs and religions.

Raised in New York City as a strict Catholic, she knows that her life, like others, had been influenced by her parent's beliefs. "You are what your parents were – in a sense. At fifty, I had an epiphany after researching other religious beliefs; I found Buddhism and meditation as a way to get closer to God. It just fits my demeanor to live in peace and harmony," Veronica says.

She has a strong belief in Karma. Now it's her turn to choose for herself and she loves the journey. "Every day is a new beginning as I reflect on this from the moment I awake each morning. I am contently seeking knowledge for myself and grateful for everything, every day," she affirms. Veronica is strong willed and intends to live a long, healthy life for the remaining of her years. She is on her spirituality walk, seeking self-exploration, as she assists her elderly parents and family members in Puerto Rico. Relaxed in knowing that God gave her the opportunity to slow down, step back, and reflect on the things that are meaningful in life; her new lifestyle has also helped her to release herself of materialistic things.

She has given away all of the possessions she accumulated over the years that seemed important to her at one time, feeling *less is better*. She says that today you will find her in a pair of sandals, and her favorite old jeans, while soaking in the sun and observing her new surroundings. Veronica looks forward to the many new passages and the enlightenment that she seeks to find in her new life path. She's not sure where the journey will lead her in terms of her next steps, but she's allowing God to lead and she knows that she is in the right place.

A New Phase In Life

MEET THIS WISE WOMAN OF COLOR:

I am Veronica Roldan-Burris, born of Hispanic descent and raised a Nuyorican. Spending most of my life in Brooklyn, New York until the tender age of twenty-five when I left to follow my heart, which landed me in the Washington metropolitan area. I'm previously married, a mother of two wonderful young adults, and a grandmother to an intuitive seven-year-old girl. I have three sisters and one brother, as well as numerous cousins, nieces and nephews. Finally, I'm a friend to the many wonderful individuals of this great universe.

After arriving in D.C., I worked for a brokerage firm for several years. Shortly afterwards, I began my twenty-five year career in Corporate America. There, I held numerous positions during my tenure. My final position as a director is one that I held with pride, being the only Hispanic woman in the company for years. My growth within the company did not come without trials and tribulations. Being a Hispanic woman required that I worked twice as hard as my fellow co-workers; however, I endured and moved on. Even though I was proud of my achievements, I never disclosed my salary to members of my family.

I come from a long line of strong, intelligent women who have endured all that life has to offer when making life choices and seeking a path to a better life. The third generation of Puerto Rican women, which includes me, depicts the strength we have learned from the women in previous generations. The only difference is that the women in my generation do not tolerate any kind of negative energy, even if it means spending your ife without a significant other. I hope that the next generation inherits the fearlessness of previous generations.

Raised a strict Catholic, I eventually I found Buddhism and meditation as a way to get closer to God, the higher being of the universe. I recently relocated to the island of Puerto Rico to live and be close to my retired parents. Finally, I bear no regrets in life; I only look forward to the many new paths and the enlightenment that I seek to find in my new life path.

28 A Change Did Come
SHELLÉE M. HAYNESWORTH

It was 2001 and she realized that she was at a point where she needed to make some changes. Her family life had changed and she was making a big move.

She had it all planned out to move on June 1, 2001 and on that day her dad died. She had just lost her stepmother a few years prior. They were both strong, supportive advocates for her and it seemed like when she lost both of them it was a reality check. Her dad was 60 and her step-mom was 55.

She doesn't know if it was in the subconscious or in her life consciousness, somehow though it inspired her and made her realize how precious life was. She was ready to come into her voice and understand who she was. She felt that she needed to listen to herself, embrace the change, and become more spiritual.

She had a huge epiphany after her dad died and just going through all of that led her to a blessing. Through the years of growing and maturing in a relationship, she hadn't recognized how much of her self she had compromised. It had been 14 years before she would look at herself in the mirror and say, *who am I today?*

It wasn't an easy decision to move forward in life after such a long time in a relationship. It seemed then like a huge move because everyone else was either married or in a relationship. She felt a certain way based off the only thing she knew and heard throughout her life: get married, get a nice guy, and get one with a job.

There was a brief time when she realized she was suffering from depression. She was operating with a little dysfunction, but persevering because as you know African American women are the mules aka backbone of our community and often times we simply just don't think about ourselves enough or at all.

Today, she is continuing to excel. She believes, "This is a good time to grow, because you can visibly see that the universe and global societies at large are changing. If we take a closer look and examine all of the current problems with the economy and in this country, we can't help but notice that things are not working." She says, "More importantly, we've been stuck in the same pattern so it's a good time for African American women to really come into themselves and hear their voices, because we are life-changers, we're influencers." Her new mantra: *change will bring fear, before it's brings faith.*

She is 48 now, and as she gets closer to 50, she finds that core values and good character have become more important to her. She's not a materialistic person so she can't relate to all of that. But, she finds that in our community, if you're not in tune with how you value your self-worthiness, you succumb to other's opinions of your self-worth; and that's where there's a disconnect. So for her, good core values are key.

Shellée grew up and lives in the D.C. area. She cherishes the life lessons and spiritual gifts that her mother continues to give to her. Her mom used to say, "We live in our own planet and we don't let others determine our worthiness." She is extremely and grateful for her mother's wisdom and spiritual guidance. She says for certain that she learned this through her mother's actions and deeds not just through her words. Her mother has always been her number one advocate and her best friend, even till this day they're extremely close. Shellée says she heard a consistent message throughout the years and she's been supported without a doubt. But, she had to mature and grow spiritually to embrace what her mom was teaching her all of these years. The year 2001, marked a major turning point for her; primarily because that was the period in her life when she began to hear and listen to her inner voice, became more open to life's possibilities, started to accept herself more as well as others, and most of all embraced her inner spirituality.

MEET THIS WISE WOMAN OF COLOR:

Shellée M. Haynesworth is an Emmy Award-winning producer, storyteller, and project manager with a long history of commitment to public media and more than 20 years of production experience. Through the years, she has produced, written, and created over 100 documentary-style programs and multimedia projects on a wide range of topics including human and civil rights, women's health, mentoring opportunities for underserved youth, community-based education and arts initiatives, and social issues and justice. Her natural ease with people fuels her storytelling abilities and results in intimate interviews with individuals ranging from CEOs to celebrities, global leaders to U.S. policymakers, and social activists to everyday people.

Shellée strategizes and executes projects with verve, blending creative vision, leadership, and an uncanny eye for detail. Her clients include the USAID, Advertising Council, HBO/Time Life Video, PBS, Black Entertainment Television, Inter-American Development Bank, Hispanic Heritage Foundation, National Association for Broadcasters (NAB), U.S. Department of Education, Academy for Educational Development (AED), National Institutes of Health, Smithsonian Institution, among others. TV production and multimedia project credits include *Latino Voices: Art and Culture* for Smithsonian Institution/PBS, *Towards Sustainable and Equitable Development: Strategies for Latin American and Caribbean Countries* for the Inter-American Development Bank, *Best Practices* for U.S. Department of Education, *Romare Bearden: The Main Ingredient* for Black Entertainment Television, *An American Reunion* for HBO/Time-Life Video, *Country Cares for St. Jude Kids* for the National Association for Broadcasters (NAB), and *Planting Hope, Harvesting Change* for the Academy for Educational Development (AED).

29 A Spiritual Awakening
VICKIE WILLIAMS

"Most of my success came as a result of my greatest disappointments. That's how I discovered that my disappointments were a catalyst for life's greatest possibilities," says Vickie.

She came to realize that her truth was her identity, and that relationships helped her realize that embracing her self-worth would help her shape that identity. After numerous failed relationships with men, she learned that she didn't owe anybody anything.

Vickie lived most of her life as a caretaker. She sought out men that needed and wanted to be rescued. She believed that it was her "absolute obligation to save African American men because of the turbulent journey they traveled on the universe." She felt it was a black woman's obligation to be there for her brothers. "They have been unjustly treated and given an incredible path to travel" – and she was compelled to be responsible for their success.

Over the years she started attracting every black man who was broken. He would either be financially broken, emotionally broken, or spiritually broken. "I was thinking that it was my job to sort of bring or herd them all in and give them a home. I did this is in several different ways, she says.

She would take care of them long enough before she looked up and there she was; she was empty. She had become the same thing that she was attempting to create in their lives. "I was this broken, empty, emotionally, spiritually deflated person."

She finally reached a point where she said, "This is not my purpose," because while she was doing that she was so very envious of women who were attracting men that were really good providers.

There she was a caretaker and one day came to realize *in order to attract a provider you have to believe that you are worthy of a provider.* Before the men ever came into her life she had predestined the relationship. "After the dissolution of the relationship with me, they would find girlfriends and wives; support their education and pay for their houses. And I was thinking wait a minute, you weren't that way with me." They would say, "That isn't what you wanted from me. You wanted to take care of me." I had to admit, "Oh yeah, I did." She had presented herself in a way that was no longer acceptable. So she had to transform how she felt about herself.

Vickie says another wakeup call was that she allowed others to speak their vision into her reality. That was particularly clear in the area of her career. "Most of my career I had been told what I could do, and it was never anything that I wanted to do, but I did it anyways because I was obedient. I thought that the individuals that were speaking to me were actually messengers. I thought that they were sent with a purpose," Vicki recalls. What she realized was that the messenger resided inside of her. She realized that there were no external messengers stronger or more significant than the messenger that lived inside of her; the one who she hadn't listen to in a really long time.

A Spiritual Awakening

"So when I began to listen to my internal messenger, that's when I began to have the greatest amount of conflict with my external messenger. I knew in that very vein that I was on to something. I've come to believe that conflict is really impetus to enlightenment. It's during those conflicting days where I've grown the most. Those are the days when I feel like I don't know, I'm not sure and the force is fighting me. But when I get through that conflict that is when the greatest amount of knowledge, spiritual enlightenment, and purpose becomes clearer. But I must get through that," Vicki strongly declares.

She is now 42, and says that the person that she is today still lives with fear, but she is willing to accept the fear and give it a seat at the table. "I now graciously excuse fear from the table verses not even believing that it was there as I did in the past. It's about knowing it's there, recognizing it's there, and graciously excusing it."

"I will admit that I used to see some of the problems I've mentioned as a curse. Now, I see them as a gift, because the gift in it is that I can't do without God or without a greater sense of self awareness."

She has had a spiritual awakening and she believes, "We all have been put on this earth in the spirit of brilliance and excellence. My advice to women is to beware of those that you surround yourself with. Who you share your dreams and vision with is so powerful. I believe this journey is not meant to be traveled alone, therefore be mindful of those you connect with because your inner circle has to be held so sacred—they will be there for you for life."

MEET THIS WISE WOMAN OF COLOR:

Williams is the executive director of the Jeremiah Program, she oversees the Minneapolis and Saint Paul Campuses. Prior to the Jeremiah Program, she worked primarily as a management consultant with a focus on organizational change and process re-engineering. Her firm worked in partnership with organizations to create results driven outcomes. She is an assistant professor at St. Catherine University, where she teaches in the Business Administration department.

She has also more than ten years of experience in sales leadership positions within Fortune 500 companies.

Williams is a 2004 Bush Foundation Leadership Fellow. She currently serves on several governing boards and volunteers with numerous community organizations. She received her Master's in Public Administration from the John F. Kennedy School of Government at Harvard University and her Bachelor of Science degree from Ithaca College in Ithaca, New York.

30 The Gift of Appreciation
JULIE FLANDERS

She's from the Virgin Islands, a small island of about 32 square miles of contentment. She grew up with her mom in the projects who did her best to raise her. She's been fortunate to always have good people around her, but she didn't always necessarily appreciate it.

Julie says her mom is definitely responsible for her foundation today. Thanks to her mother, she is very assertive and a go getter. Like many youth she has spent her life determined to prove her mother wrong. Her mom was a tough-love kind of mother and Julie thought it was frustrating growing up, because they weren't as close as she liked them to be.

The epiphany came when she was 27 years old. She had just purchased her first home in Virginia and her mom was coming to visit. Julie was a bit anxious hoping that her mom would be proud of her. Julie's life had been planned to the tee and so far she was ahead of her schedule. She planned her life up until the age of 30. She knew by then that she would have a house, a car, and her bachelor's degree. Little did she know she would have her master's degree by then, too. She was excited to see her mom when she arrived. Her mom was so proud of her and that's when she realized how much she loved her. Hearing her approval made all the difference. It was then that she came to understand all that her mom had done for her with the little she had. Her mom just wanted her to have the best and to be a better person than she was. Her mom told her, "The only thing I wanted for you was for you to be a good person, and you've done that. I am so proud of you." Julie credits her mom for being the driving force for everything she is.

She says she is thankful to many that have blessed her along the way and helped her to succeed. Although life has been good, she says she didn't know her worth until she was around the age of 21. It was then that a white woman, named Danelle took her in as her own to live with her family. It was her last semester in undergraduate school and she was just finishing her four year scholarship for basketball. Julie wanted badly to play volleyball after graduating and she really didn't want to go back to the Virgin Islands at the time. She says volleyball had always been her dream sport, but she was put into a basketball world.

During a conversation with Danelle, a woman she hardly knew, she was offered an opportunity to stay so she could continue on with school. She remembers thinking, "What is wrong with this woman, that she would want a 6'3" black chick to stay with her?" She was wondering what was up with that. This just wasn't normal to her. She spoke with her coach who was one of her biggest mentors at the time. Her coach asked her the same thing, "What's wrong with her?" Julie just said that she didn't know. It was the least unexpected for her to see a Caucasian woman be so kind and open doors to her, a complete stranger. To hear Danelle tell it, she didn't have a tint in her skin. When she told her mom, there were no worries because mom felt it seemed like a good environment to stay in. In her Virgin Island accent mom said, "Iz ah good ting yuh modah always so good to peepull, cause yuh see wha' happen wen yuh good to peepull, good tings duz happen." Julie laughed because her mom made it all about her.

The Gift of Appreciation

Julie felt like a magnet to good things. That year she played volleyball on a 5th year scholarship and she stayed with Danelle, her two other daughters and their dog. She would be there until the semester ended. Upon completion of the semester, she opted to give the remainder of her scholarship to another deserving student who really needed it. In a discussion with her coach, it was then that the idea of going overseas to play basketball became a possibility. She never thought it was an option, but she became thrilled by the thought. She talked it over with Danelle who had now become 'Momma' and she was told to go because she was young, it was an awesome opportunity, and she had her whole life ahead to fulfill. She left for Finland that December leaving behind her things at home; Momma's house. She lived in Spain and Finland during her two-year tour coming home to visit the family during breaks.

As time had passed and she was nearing her return home, she began to feel that she was getting older and she needed to figure out what was next for her life. She was feeling the need to be more independent. She knew she wanted to pursue her master's degree at some point. Julie decided to retire from professional basketball and applied to graduate school at George Mason. Upon her arrival from her last stint in Finland, Momma got her into a marketing position where Julie gave basketball one last shot. Julie attended a tryout session for the WNBA. She was invited to training camp, which lasted a week. She felt she couldn't wait for a decision to be made; she needed to make money and graduate school would be starting in the fall.

A year and a half passed by and by now Julie had a few great jobs and she went on to pursue her master's degree, she was around 23-24 years old. It was during her second semester of graduate school when her mentor, the coach, gave her a surprise call. He notified her of an open position to be an assistant coach at Howard University. She took the job and says that job helped her on her journey in discovering her worth.

By now Julie was ready to move out and take a step toward further defining her independence. She spoke to Momma about being ready and weighed all options to ensure that she was ready. Momma blessed her with a $10,000 deposit for her new home. She says she was adopted into a situation where they didn't need, and would help whenever they could help. At first she was reluctant to take the help because she believed that they must have wanted something in return. She knew she was conditioned to believe that every time someone does something for you it had a price. But, she had to learn to put a price on herself so that no one along the way that had helped her would ever be disappointed for doing so. Julie says that she didn't understand the appreciation that people had for her; therefore she couldn't appreciate what she brought to everyone else. She pushed herself extra and did her best to make them all proud. She has been nicknamed by the players and colleagues, The General and Judge Julie, respectively. She says we must be responsible for our own actions. *If we're not prepared for tomorrow, then how can we be ready for right now?*

The lesson for Julie was that others sometimes believe in you just because the human condition allows us to believe in that which is not always tangible. People sometimes see promise in you and have the ability to give, whether it's as a mentor, in gifts or love. In her case she didn't value herself enough to feel worthy of accepting the gift of mere appreciation. It took years for her to realize that her families of supporters were her angels, along with her mother, who had the courage and love to let her go so she could have better. Julie loves to go to her homes to visit today. She says she was granted two mothers for a reason that cannot be explained and couldn't ask for more.

MEET THIS WISE WOMAN OF COLOR:

"Our voices are all we have, but are often wasted unless we have the courage to be heard. Speak up for not what you believe in, but from where your faith lies." - Julie F.

I heard once that if you wake up every morning and you want to do a particular thing, then that's who you are. I'm a writer. All I want to do is write. I hope to one day inspire the world to be better so that we can do better. My inspiration to write stems from my fascination with our human condition. We naively get lost in ourselves not recognizing that our actions affect others around us – directly or indirectly (global warming, worldwide recessions, etc.). This is the flaw and the beauty of the human condition.

Let's not be confused: I'm not Gandhi or MLK Jr.; just Julie F. However, with every new opportunity I have been given to take a breath and be a witness, it becomes more and more clear that we, as individuals, should be nowhere near where we were yesterday.

I am a bit of a perfectionist who knows either all or nothing. My philosophy being, "Aim for Perfection so that even when we fall short, we are still good enough."

My being is not about me, but about the influence I leave on others around, and after me. My parents, Caucasian and my birth mother, French West Indian, have given me a foundation from where I have been able to find myself in my own identity and if I can help another individual be an intellectual among the conformed minds of today's society then my task is complete. The biggest failure we could ever experience is an epiphany of a truth turned lie: I like to argue that many of us think we know what we know only because we have been conditioned to believe what we know is so.

Oh, and did I mention, I'm a bit of a philosopher too? All in all, I'm just big on communication.

~ Julie

31 She's Telling It
BEV JOHNSON

"I would like to believe that I am a woman of God, a servant." All throughout her days, Bev finds herself ministering to people and helping them to listen to their hearts. She speaks life to people through her voice (a voice of soul), which is a gift from God in the form of a singing blessing.

She comes across several people who are questioning their purpose, or seeking a deeper connection, and when she does, she tells them, "Embrace it and just go with what God places in your heart. There is nothing in our life that God doesn't see, know and allow. He lets us go down certain journeys to get us where we need to be. If you look at the story of Moses in the Bible and Noah who was a common man with issues, you will see that he was obedient to God in seeing through the vision to build the Ark when no else would listen. God continued blessing him because of his obedience."

"I see myself and millions of other women in a way where we may not have a doctorate of theology but, we were called to serve." She says that God will send you the message in mysterious ways over and over again. She remembers when He would send her messages in her sleep and then one day while in church He told her to raise up and praise. "It was powerful, so much so that I started choking. It was a dry heaving choke. That was when I said to Jesus, so be it and I moved forward with the vision of a music ministry." My praise, My Worship Music & Arts Ministry was born.

"I will admit that getting started was not easy. I had many trials along the way. You name it, it occurred; from people who were envious, to financial challenges, to having to obtain permissions, and even family health issues surfaced. I pushed through it all, because God assured me that these were just tests." Until now, she hadn't mentioned anyone other than family, but she has a slight case of dyslexia, where she sometimes reads and spells backwards. She could sing anything, but was afraid to read and speak aloud. Joking with confidence, her answer to that is "You know what? That's what they have spell check for."

"To any woman reading this story I say to you to remember that when God gives you an assignment and someone comes up against you, to remember that they are elevating you. When I went through my journey, the adversities made me more determined than ever. For me to succeed through it, I put fire and energy behind it. Out of it came my purpose in life and I couldn't be more blessed by it.

No matter what the world may say, I give Him praise."

MEET THIS WISE WOMAN OF COLOR:

"I don't have a PhD in theology or masters in music, but what I do have is the gift of the Holy Spirit. For me that is much more valuable than silver or gold."

God has placed within all of us gifts and talents that will enable us to be successful in life. These gifts give us a clue to the plans that God has for us. He desires that we use these gifts to glorify Him, to be successful in life, and to be a significant blessing to others. Proverbs 18:16

She's Telling It

Bev Johnson, gospel recording artist/songwriter is known for her evangelistic, anointed voice throughout Northern Virginia for setting the atmosphere for praise and worship through song. She accepted Jesus Christ as her personal Savior at the age of eight and has been singing traditional and contemporary gospel ever since.

Beverly has opened up with praise and worship at numerous churches across Northern Virginia, as well as in her hometown Dallas, Texas. She has provided back-up vocals for the late Orlando Draper, along with the "Voices of Faith" (Clarksville, TN), Bobby Jones (Nashville, TN), and evangelist Beverly Crawford. Bev has opened up for several gospel artists who include Maurette Brown Clark, Lonnie Hunter, and Juan Santiago & Uninhibited Praise.

In February 2009, Bev recorded her first gospel CD, titled "My Praise, My Worship." The CD was released September 7, 2009. She is the founder and minister of music for My Praise, My Worship Music & Arts Ministry, which consists of singing, praise dancing, sign language and mime. Bev Johnson, My Praise, My Worship Music & Arts Ministry hosts an annual "Praise and Worship" workshop and concert featuring top college gospel choirs including Virginia Commonwealth University's "Black Awakening Gospel Choir" and Virginia State University's gospel choir, along with dynamic artists in the District of Columbia, Northern Virginia, and Maryland area.

ACKNOWLEDGEMENTS

This book would not have been possible without the help of numerous *angels in disguise* – too many to mention, including mentors, contributors, supporters, friends and family. Among the many mentors who have contributed to my thinking and understanding of self-worth and value, I extend my thanks to the following people: My Mom, Patricia Hameed, Dad, Clinton Leon Jones (deceased), Rev. Phil M. Turner, Pastor for spiritual leadership and support, Dr. Amardo Rodriguez for nurturing the seed in 2002, and Rev. Daren C. Jaime for lifting me up and pushing me forward.

For unselfish acts of contributing kindness, I give a *high praise* to: Craig Boothe for believing in me, Richy Rolon for continuous encouragement, and Chef Will Lewis for his spiritual ear and unconditional guidance.

Without a doubt, thank you to my family. Special acknowledgement to my daughter, India B'nai Dancil; irreplaceable love to Grandma Betty Morrow, Brother R. Abdul H., and Sister Naimah H.; big hug to Aunt Janet, Uncle Freddie Thomas, Ashiea (Niki) Hammonds, Dujuan Hammonds-*Son of Ian*, Aunt LeVore Freeman, Nyelle Hameed and the rest of the ATL crew.

I am sincerely grateful to the giving spirit of 30 amazing women whose time, heart and spirit were priceless – thank you for taking this journey with me. To my other Sistas in Christ, thank you for your unbending support.

She's Telling It

To my professional services team; I am gracious for the tireless efforts of Ali Shaun Collins, IAM Global Media, Inc. and for his role in preparing countless artwork designs for the cover, advertisements, and business presence. I also thank LaVergne Harden Photography for her *keen eye* (cover photo) and editor, Sonda Denise Roberts, for her patience and editing prowess.

TOPICS

For discussion purposes a list of topics covered throughout the book have been listed.

CAREER
Education
Entrepreneurship
Personal Development
Professional
   Development
Unemployment

FAMILY
Divorce
Marriage
Parenting
Relationships
Support

GUIDANCE
Coach
Counselor
History
Leadership
Mentor
Ministry
Politics
Sisterhood

HARDSHIP
Emotional
Financial
Physical
Spiritual

HEALTH & WELLNESS
Abuse
Abandonment
Addiction
Advocate
Autism
Alzheimer's disease
Autism
Cancer
Caregiver
Depression
Disability
Dyslexia
Exercise
Faith
Grief
Homeless

Living Fast/
   Dangerously
Mental Illness
Perseverance
Rape
Spirituality
Validation
Values
Worth

ABOUT THE AUTHOR

Nasha L. Barnes is a 2012 Central New York National Organization for Women (NOW) Awardee, motivational speaker, and leadership trainer. She is the Owner and CEO of Aim Higher Enterprises™, a consulting company based in Syracuse, New York. Realizing early in her youth that those in need of visionary direction were drawn to her, she began to fulfill her life's purpose of assisting others to find outlets to their current situations – she offered vision and the willingness to dream beyond existing boundaries. It is her dream to share and spread the blessing of vision, reaching as many as possible in need of encouragement and empowerment in both social and economic advancement.

Ms. Barnes has been recognized for her specialty of helping women overcome transitions in life. She founded her ministry Women Aim Higher in 2011; today her ministry is reaching women in congregations across the country training them on business, personal and professional development. She is also the founder of Kidz Aim Higher, a youth mentoring program designed to elevate the vision of girls.

Nasha speaks and conducts workshops inspiring people with her passion and spreading an insightful message of heightened vision. Her diverse upbringing allows her to communicate with people from all walks of life; including women of faith, single mothers, at risk youth, students, professionals, and companies seeking diversity and inclusion. She is also an advocate for social, political, and economic causes. She lives her life with passion and purpose; desiring to empower others with the ability to be fearless with character.

CPSIA information can be obtained at www.ICGtesting.com
Printed in the USA
BVOW060144050412

286902BV00002B/2/P